What People Are Saying abo

"Carolyn's words cut through the popular light-washed self-help and spiritual canon, offering deep soul relief and a celebration that warmly invites our shadows to be unleashed from closets shrouded by shame. Beyond soul relief, Carolyn shows us that our spiritual growth and magical practices can be deeply fun even in their slimiest iteration. Her skillful way of teaching ancient tantra and alchemy that we can access without robes, mantras, or gurus is a gift."

—Alexandra Roxo, author of
F*ck Like a Goddess: Heal Yourself.
Reclaim Your Voice. Stand in Your Power.

"Elliott, in this evocative debut, encourages the exploration of taboo desires hidden within the unconscious mind. Elliott uses the Jungian concept of the shadow to posit that repressed and denied aspects of oneself manifest in negative ways, and she moves on to argue that individuals, on an unconscious level, can enjoy these feelings, and 'get off' on the 'forbidden enjoyment' they bring to one's shadow. Her meditation method (existential kink) is presented as a radical, somatic, hot, immediately practical and quick method to bring these patterns to light, therefore dismantling them by tapping into one's unconscious mind and soul-spirit realms through meditative and spell-casting practices. Elliott's novel methods could help spiritual readers looking to bring more positivity into their lives."

—*Publishers Weekly*

"I have a confession to make. There are some painful stories of my past that I have held on to for far too long. It never made sense on the surface. Why would I obsess over these situations? Why can't I just let them go? Carolyn Elliott's *Existential Kink* provided the answer that I've been searching for all these years: on some level, I 'got off' on these sad stories. Playing martyr felt good. When I began applying the practices in this book, I was able to turn around that thinking and release those trauma tales once and for all. This book will challenge you to look at your shadow side in a new way. Instead of ignoring it or covering up the old scars with 'love and light,' you'll learn how to find power in the darkness. When you do that, a funny thing happens: you're free."

—Theresa Reed, author of *Astrology For Real Life:*
A No B.S. Guide for the Astro-Curious

"This is shadow integration made practical and completely understandable. *No* one else explains shadow integration in such a way that it makes solid sense. It can be so difficult to embrace parts of your being that you've been rejecting your entire life let alone see those parts. But I *love* that Carolyn finds a way to poetically and articulately explain why it's so important *and* that she teaches *how* to do it in simple stages!"

—Akhera Unpa Shepsutera

"It straight up works. The Existential Kink method is effective in bringing emotions up and out. I finally have a tool that takes the mystery out of any emotion. Emotions are no longer torturous devices that stick around forever."

—Ellen Garbarino

"Existential Kink is such a liberating approach to seeing and facing my dramas and traumas. The way it twists my victimhood into strengths, debilitating my blame reactions, is maddening and now unstoppable. I am facing myself better. I am seeing my self-pity and reactivity in new light. I am much closer to taking *full* responsibility for my life. And I am doing all that with a lighter heart and a lack of self-loathing."

—Moira Lowe

"I admit that I am still learning to celebrate and 'get off' on the fuckups instead of the old knee-jerk reaction of disappointment. It's definitely a mind-twister but *oh my god*, it is such an exponentially more fun and fulfilling way to go through life!"

—Michelle Lewis

Existential Kink

A method for getting what you want by getting off on what you don't

Existential
Kink

UNMASK YOUR SHADOW AND EMBRACE YOUR POWER

Carolyn Elliott, PhD

WEISER
BOOKS

This edition first published in 2020 by Weiser Books, an imprint of
Red Wheel/Weiser, LLC
With offices at:
65 Parker Street, Suite 7
Newburyport, MA 01950
www.redwheelweiser.com

ISBN: 978-1-57863-647-1

Library of Congress Cataloging-in-Publication Data available upon request.

Cover photograph by Rolfo / Moment / Getty Images
Interior illustrations by Eroshka / Shutterstock
Typeset in Aller Light

Printed in Canada
MAR
10 9 8 7 6 5

Dedications

To all the participants of my online courses INFLUENCE, FORCE OF NATURE, MONEY, LOVE, and THRILL—thank you for your depths of honesty and commitment to this wild work; it's a beacon and a joy to me.

To my coven-mates Crystal Woodling, Annie Derek, Angela Morelli, Carolyn Burns, Alyssa Schlumpf, thank you for all the encouragement, wisdom, strong medicine, and big belly laughs.

To my husband, David Lee Elliott (aka Taia Kepher), thank you for driving me crazy in all the best, freakiest, and most magical ways.

Contents

Preface: What Is Existential Kink? xiii

Prologue: The Underworld Mystery
(*revisited in all its shadow*) xix

Part One: Existential Basics 3

An Introduction to the Shadow
(*and why it's such an unconscious turn-on*) 5

The Unconscious 15

Lesson 1: Super-Freak Divine Alchemy **23**

Lesson 2: The Seven Axioms of Existential Kink **39**

Lesson 3: "EK"—The Basic Practice **51**

INTERLUDE
Stories of Transformative Experiences 71

Part Two: Getting Kinky 83

Projection 85

Lesson 4: "EK" Exercises for Transformative Magic **89**

INTERLUDE
More Stories of Transformative Experiences 167

Part Three: Questions and Answers 179

Appendix 195

What Is Existential Kink?

A provocative title—but what exactly does it mean? Existential Kink is an amazing, rapid shadow-integration process that I developed over many years of teaching my courses; a process that I've used again and again to help my coaching clients and course participants get astounding results. That is what this book is about—sharing that process with you.

Existential Kink is a specific meditative practice that I teach that's all about dissolving negative patterns by being willing to uncover and celebrate the previously unconscious pleasure that we actually—paradoxically—derive from those "yucky" patterns.

And to be clear: by negative patterns I mean common troubles like:

- Not being able to make more than a certain smallish amount of money each month, no matter how hard you try

- Perpetually dating people who end up bearing an uncanny resemblance to one of your abusive parents

- Feeling stuck with certain health or weight conditions

- Having intuitive or creative blocks

These are the kinds of things that tend to afflict all of us at some point, if we're honest. And if we're extra, super-honest—honest on a level below our usual awareness—we all take a freaky, kinky, sado-masochistic delight in our afflictions, which is why we end up with them again and again.

This notion is by no means entirely new. I earned a doctorate in Critical and Cultural Studies at the University of Pittsburgh, and along the way I read a lot of psychology. My deep dive into psychology taught me that we human beings have a major habit of taking unconscious pleasure in the "bad stuff" in our lives. This was well-known to the founding giants of psychology like Freud, Jung, and Lacan. Freud called it "psychic masochism," Jung recognized it as "the Shadow," and Lacan called it *jouissance*—pleasure that's so intense we repress it.

All of these psychologists recognized that a major component of helping people involved getting them to acknowledge and "own" this kind of weird underlying *desire* for and *pleasure in* stuff that they ostensibly hate and feel very frustrated by.

It's strange, but it's true. Jung said—and I'll repeat it a few times throughout this book—"Until you make the unconscious, conscious, it will rule your life and you will call it Fate."

He was absolutely right about that.

In other words, as long as we have unconscious (repressed, denied, disowned) enjoyment in some "bad" thing in our lives, we will keep seeking out that very same "bad" thing; we'll perpetuate it without even realizing that we're doing so.

I learned first-hand that by embracing my "psychic masochism," by recognizing and empowering the darkness of my "shadow," and in the end taking "pleasure" in my yucky stuff that I could do something amazing. I could completely integrate my "good" self with my "bad" self and become a whole person. Healed.

Applying this insight to my own life, I found I rapidly dissolved patterns of poverty, bad relationships, and health and creativity problems that had plagued me for over a decade.

This insight is what's involved in "shadow work." And it's not for the faint of heart.

However, this insight is rarely discussed in pop psychology and self-help books, which tend to focus on "Love & Light" (repeated affirmations, visualizations, positivity, etc.) and many people are frustrated when this approach does not produce results. What I had learned—and what Existential Kink teaches—is that the key to a magical life rests in delving into the other end of the spectrum: finding the power of the darkness.

One of my course participants describes it in this perfect analogy:

> I realized that when you only focus on the light and positive thinking . . . then it's like you're staring up at the sun without looking down to notice that you were standing in a pile of feces.
>
> Something smells bad, but as long as you stare at the light then all the bad will go away.
>
> And instead of cleaning up the poo you spray perfume (affirmations) all over it.
>
> Meanwhile, shadow work is looking down at the shit so you can clean it up or even compost it into a lush garden.

The Existential Kink method means looking inside, into the unconscious, into your fears and triggers and pain, to admit you actually take freaky joy in standing in that pile of shit.

This is an insight that can be very, very offensive to our egos: the idea that on some level we could want or enjoy "awful" things in our lives is scary and troubling to most people.

We tend to think we only want or enjoy "good" things, or that we *should* only want "good" things.

But acknowledging our secret bliss in "the bad stuff" doesn't have to be a troubling recognition; it's just a normal part of human nature. We all do it, and there doesn't need to be any shame or blame in it at all.

In fact, setting aside shame and blame is what allows us to make the enjoyment *conscious*, and thereby lets us remove its power to sneakily control us.

So scary or not, I'm making the argument that this is a very important insight to integrate into how we live our lives. In fact, through my online courses, I've helped thousands of people dramatically turn their lives around by teaching them how to do this, so it's a subject dear to my heart. The Existential Kink meditation and attitude have done wonders for them, and throughout this book, you'll read some stories of their experiences, their rapid successes, and you'll recognize the issues as very similar to your own.

The very good news is, the minute that we're willing to make that previously unconscious pleasure a *conscious* one—-the minute we're willing to deliberately celebrate it and savor it—we create a massive pattern interrupt.

We allow ourselves to finally receive the "dark secret joy" we've been (unbeknownst to ourselves!) seeking.

We let the desire that motivated the negative pattern be fully known and satisfied, and then we're free to move beyond it and create something new.

That's what this book, *Existential Kink*, is all about.

In my own life, I have practiced consciously, deliberately allowing myself to feel those intense sensations, which previously I had labeled as "anxiety, humiliation," and I noticed those feelings came with flushed cheeks and faster heartbeat—arousal.

"Fear is excitement without the breath," as Fritz Perls said. Well, often sensations that we experience as terrible or painful are just pleasure without approval.

I realized, for example, that my poverty gave me arousal. On a physical level, if I felt that arousal without judging it, it gave me pleasure.

As Milton said, "The mind is its own place, and in itself can make a Heaven of Hell, a Hell of Heaven."

Well, I decided to make a Heaven of my Hell.

The end result turned my life around.

• • •

Here it's important to acknowledge that every difficult thing in life—whether it's poverty, racism, sexism, or relationship, health, or creativity issues due to childhood wounds—all of these obviously are not solely individual inventions. None of us individually invented these "dark secret desires" for painful things in our lives, and none of us is individually, solely responsible for the fact that they exist, or that we experience them. There are things that go beyond the individual, that are part of the mass "collective shadow" (as Jung would put it).

For example, the poverty that I experienced for years wasn't my single-handed creation. It had to do with systemic, collective issues of sexism and corporatism, no doubt. But the thing is, me wailing about sexism and corporatism (which I *loved* to do, I *loved* to go to protests like Occupy and to righteously post on Facebook about all the injustices affecting me) never did a damn thing to alter the bare fact of my lack of funds, or my suffering.

Nor did it really alter the situation for anyone else, as far as I could tell.

The only thing that changed my life was me becoming willing to look at my *existential kink*: my previously unconscious desire for what I experienced—to look at it, own it, embrace it, and accept the *jouissance.* And this let me become much more creative, happy, and healthy, and to help others to do the same.

I believe that the same is true for anyone who's willing to do this work. You might be up against some very big, very painful societal or familial setbacks, and yet when you become willing to really excavate your previously unconscious role in your difficult situation, you gain exactly the freedom, courage, and creativity that you need to overcome those setbacks and to even lift up other people.

No one else can grow or heal or have a realization of your own paradoxical, wonderful kinkiness for you.

The Underworld Mystery
(revisited in all its shadow)

There's an ancient Greek story in which the King of the Underworld, Pluto, kidnaps and rapes the maiden goddess Persephone. You're probably familiar with it, but to refresh your memory, it goes a little something like this:

Young Persephone is hanging out in the meadows picking flowers one lovely Olympian day and suddenly the earth rips open under her feet, a menacing man appears, grabs her, takes her down into the blackness of the Underworld, rapes her, marries her, and then tricks her into eating pomegranate seeds—Underworld food—so that she can never totally leave him, and she herself becomes the Queen of the Underworld.

It's a sad, awful story of kidnapping, rape, control, violence, and abuse.

Yet.

For thousands of years it never occurred to anyone in Greece that there might be a *King* of the Underworld; there was just a Queen of the Underworld. Digging down into the most ancient layer of myth before the Persephone saga, there existed "She Who Destroys the Light." Similar to the Hindu goddess Kali, Persephone was worshipped as the Goddess of Death.

So long before there was Pluto, there was Persephone, alone.

Persephone was a maiden goddess in the sense that she was undivided, complete, whole-unto-herself. She was called Kore, which means "maiden" but also "core, heart." She was understood to be the core, the heart, the essence of everything.

The tale of Pluto and the Rape of Persephone was a later invention; it came thousands of years after the first celebrations of the goddess.

What should we make of that?

What I make of it is this:

Pluto is himself an unconscious aspect of the Kore's (Persephone's) divinity.

In modern astrology, Pluto represents the Unconscious Divine: all of those vast forces of death and terror and rape and evil and destruction and hoarding of wealth. In other words, all the terrible things in this world that we habitually refuse to identify with and to take personal responsibility for in order to maintain our feeling of being "regular" ego selves.

Pluto also represents the possibility of alchemy itself, the deliberate, miraculous transformations that become available when the powers of the Unconscious Divine are recognized, remembered, embraced, forgiven, loved, and made conscious.

The way I see it, one day the great Kore got bored with being the solitary, boundlessly powerful ruler of the Underworld. She decided she wanted some drama to break up the eternal monotony of being complete-unto-herself, omniscient, and omnipotent.

So, the Kore split in two: she created a benevolent, sweet, conscious self and a vicious, unconscious divine twin, Pluto.

She split in order to experience herself as a separate, innocent individual—a perpetual little girl picking flowers in a meadow—AND, then to subsequently have the super-edgy, kinky experience of duality and sexuality and violence and all the terrifying thrills and chills that come with it.

The Kore desired to experience a great story, and in a great story, whether comedy or tragedy, there are always struggle and obstacles and opposition. There are separation and reunion.

From this angle, the Rape of Persephone is the story of the singular divine choosing to create duality and then having a horrible, painful experience of itself and then ultimately returning to sovereignty, to union, this time with a self-awareness that can only come from having experienced itself as terrifyingly Other.

Pluto is everything we experience as Other (which is to say "out there" in the great "not me" of the world), that's too horrible and too vast and sublime and violent to personally identify with.

In the public version of the Greek myth that has come down to us through the ages, after being kidnapped by Pluto, Persephone is ever-after a sad and unwilling Queen of the Underworld. Because she ate those damned (literally) pomegranate seeds, she can only spend six months of the year with her mother Demeter in the sunny fields of Olympus, and the rest of the time she's sentenced to the Underworld, surrounded by ghosts, married to her torturer.

This version of the myth isn't very magically inspiring, however, is it?

So I think there's reason to suspect that the "real story" of the Rape of Persephone, perhaps the one that was revealed to participants in the Mysteries of Eleusis—the highly secretive, great magic school of Ancient Greece—is something much closer to this:

Persephone suffers through her ordeal (kidnap, rape, control) and then one night, deep in reflection on her miserable fate, she eats the food of the Underworld, seeds from a pomegranate. When she eats the seeds, she accepts the Underworld back into herself (literally ingests it) and remembers that she herself created Pluto by her own choice in order to experience herself as separate and innocent. It's an "aha" moment. As Persephone remembers this, she sees Pluto in a new light.

Instead of seeing a cruel monster, she sees a lover so selfless, so devoted, and so subservient, that he fully played the role of a malicious villain just because she asked him to. Seeing this, Persephone forgives Pluto and they tenderly unite.

Persephone goes on to reign as Queen of the Underworld, this time no longer bored and alone, but now with a devoted lover, and with full awareness of her power and all the responsibility it entails. This is an awareness that could only come by experiencing her own power as *Other*.

The Underworld Mystery is this: Pluto, the Unconscious Divine, hateful as he seems, is in truth our own creation, a kind and devoted lover, and that all the vast power of Pluto becomes available to us when we remember this, forgive him, take responsibility for our own experience of his power (which was really ours all along), and love him.

We all embody duality—we all have both light (conscious) and dark (unconscious) dimensions of our being. The dark side of our personality—the "other," the shadow side, is dark not only because we don't (or won't) see it; it's dark because it's comprised of what we would consider our primitive, primal, or negative impulses—all of which we choose to keep hidden from our consciousness, and denied. And like Persephone, our goal is to become whole.

Becoming whole means we recognize our dark, kinky side, and that we not only accept it, forgive it, and take responsibility for it, but that we *love* it, enjoy its antics, and finally integrate it into our whole being.

And that is the source of true power. That is transformative magic.

Existential

Part One

Existential Basics

"Until you make the unconscious,
conscious, it will rule your life
and you will call it Fate."

—CARL JUNG

An Introduction to the Shadow
(and why it's such an unconscious turn-on)

What if, deep within you, you had a never-ending reservoir of wrongness?

Like, what if deep down inside, everything about you was totally detestable, dangerous, a source of pain to yourself and other people?

And what if that was *absolutely great*?

I'm asking these strange questions because I've noticed that pretty much all of us human beings who aren't completely enlightened (so: the population of earth minus Eckhart Tolle, Byron Katie, the Dalai Lama, and some humble shamans who lack PR agents), all of us feel, at some level, that there's something unbearably deficient, horrible, ugly, and lacking about ourselves that we need to cover over (to hide, to bury, to run from) and we cover it over with accomplishment, with the approval of others, or with black tar heroin.

I feel this sense of shameful wrongness at times. Maybe you don't feel it at all. Maybe you're free—in which case, kudos! You are very welcome to close this book and go about your enlightened life, my friend. But back to the rest of us living with the affliction of a nagging sense that we're "not okay" . . .

This awful "not okay" feeling can be exacerbated by just about anything: a grouchy tone from our partner, a withering look from our boss, the news that our high school nemesis just won the Pulitzer Prize. Many of us are able to keep this repulsive, monstrous feeling of shameful inadequacy out of sight and out of mind in order to go about the business of being relatively functional adults.

Yet a significant number of folks find it necessary to numb and hide this sense of wrongness by using every available form of addiction—from social media to workaholism to porn to alcohol and drugs—all to keep it shushed up. Some other folks are just completely taken over and paralyzed by their awareness of the wrongness. Among these we might count those with severe depression or other mental illness. Some end up committing suicide.

Even those in the "functional adult" camp with relatively mild addictive tendencies often find that despite their best efforts and intentions, dark patterns repeat in their lives. And repeat. Maybe these functional adults have plenty of happy, fulfilling things going on in their lives but they can't ever seem to make more than a certain amount of money each month, or over and over again they choose intimate partners who bear a striking resemblance to their abusive parent. Somehow, one way or another, for the majority of us humans—whether it's through our addictions or through our lousy patterns, our hidden sense of wrongness makes itself felt.

So a question arises: *what the fuck are we gonna do about this?*

I say: let's transmute that feeling of "wrongness" into raw, hot, glorious power.

Let me tell you a little story.

When I was in my twenties, I spent a lot of time sitting in moldy church basements in my hometown of Pittsburgh, Pennsylvania, listening to people talk about surrendering to God. As it happens, I was not, at that time, a dedicated basement-loving Christian; I was a misfit attending 12-step groups to help me recover from heroin addiction.

I was doing this whole recovery thing while also going to school to get a doctorate in Critical and Cultural Studies. Getting a doctorate in Critical and Cultural Studies entails reading an awful lot of weird existential philosophy, like the works of Kierkegaard and Heidegger and Nietzsche and Sartre. As I listened every night at my 12-step meetings to dozens of stories of devastation and redemption in the mildew-y air, I also thought about my own painful life experiences. As a little child, I was molested by a man I dearly loved—so that was a real head-trip which eventually made narcotics seem like a GREAT idea. And as I listened to these people "let go and let God," one distinct thought gradually formed in my mind:

God is one kinky-ass motherfucker.

God—the divine—whatever He/She/IT is—creates this world, and this world is a gonzo horror show of war and rape and abuse and addiction and disaster.

*If God is running the show, God must **like** it this way!*

Now, you might guess that a thought like that would lead to some kind of terrible nihilistic breakdown. But for me . . . actually, it didn't. Instead, it made me smile—perversely—and gave me a feeling of lightness, play, and possibility. Because I had also stumbled upon this further thought: maybe I'm one freaky-ass motherfucker too! What if—seriously *what if*—all the bad stuff had manifested in my life because I *like it that way*?

Here is a profound example.

At the time, I was in a physically abusive relationship with a jealous, controlling guy. I had met this guy through a Craigslist personal ad because I was having such a tough time finding someone to date. (Yes, I know how that sounds. Yes, it was *that* bad, and yes, I was *that* messed up.) I knew the relationship was damaging and crazy and dangerous, but I just couldn't seem to *let it go*. I would break up with the guy, send him packing, and then call him with a seductive phone call the next day.

Then he'd come back, there'd be some nice kissing, and within minutes we'd be back to yelling and he'd be throwing things at me (coffee mugs, books, etc.).

I *hated* how controlling and violent my partner was.

And yet, after much inquiry and reflection, I realized I actually *loved* how controlling and violent he was.

Loved, loved, *loved it.* I *adored* the feeling of being important that came from having this guy treat me like I was a supply of heroin that he had to manage in order to have it available at all times.

In other words, my existence had meaning.

Just as in the tale of Persephone and Pluto, I could use him to keep me contained, so that I didn't have to risk exploring myself or the world without him.

Part of what kept me hooked into the relationship was the joy of resenting him and his controlling violence. Another part of what kept me hooked in was the feeling that I could *only* have this terrible relationship because *I* was terrible, and if I could just become un-terrible, *then* I could leave him. But as long as I was terrible, I might as well stay with him, because even though he's possessive and violent, he's more entertaining than being alone. So I tried to become an un-terrible person, but that didn't work. The very act of trying to be un-terrible generally makes one more certain that one is terrible.

This scenario I've described is a looney type of bondage, a system of imposed constriction, which I had been using to keep myself from facing the great unknown. It finally occurred to me that the logic of "I can only get this terrible relationship because I am terrible" was *not true.* Rather the following realization was true:

I have this terrible relationship because my unconscious *secretly likes* feeling maniacally controlled by an evil outside agency.

As I let the realization sink in that the ugliness in my life was there not because it was somehow *necessary* or *true* but just because a shadowy part of me liked it—a giant space opened up in my body. I allowed myself to consciously feel the previously unconscious pleasure I felt in being violently controlled. It was in fact a previously unconscious turn-on. My "aha" moment.

Turn-on is magnetic. Now I was faced with the stark realization that I had been unconsciously magnetizing abuse and scarcity and rejection to myself all my life.

It occurred to me that I had been unconsciously enjoying and magnetizing self-devaluation for years, but I had never before let myself know it because it's a shameful, freaky, weird thing to be turned on by devaluation and scarcity in real life.

I mean, in sophisticated circles it's totally cool to be turned on by devaluation in some spicy S&M bedroom scene—but in real life? That's just fucked up.

And then it dawned on me: Shit, I don't just have bedroom kink, I have *existential* kink. I have perverse desires for pain and bondage in my *daily existence*.

So in my desperate twenties, in that mildew-y basement, among those sharing and willing to let God take the responsibility for all the pain, sadness, and fucked-up-ness of their lives, I came up with the following thought:

Well if God is a kinky freak and I'm a part of God like all these "spiritual" people say, maybe deep down I'm a kinky freak too.

And maybe I can get more in touch with my divine nature by giving myself permission to like all the scary stuff in life, instead of just resenting it.

This realization—embracing my *existential* kink—became the foundation of a long inquiry into the nature of consciousness and divinity and creation that is the source of all the immense good things in my life today.

And in my life today there are many very good things. A truly loving, hot husband. A seven-figure business. World travel. A circle of genuine friends. An ever-growing spiritual connection. An insane level of beauty and bounty that sometimes still staggers me, given I came from a childhood of poverty, molestation, and addiction. (And yes, in my life today there's also still a goodly share of self-created pain and suffering—because at times I still enjoy the drama of generating that suffering for myself—but I'm able to recognize it for what it is.)

My exploration of what I call my Existential Kink has changed my life.

This book is the result of that exploration. I wrote it because I want as many other people as possible to experience the kind of huge turnaround in life and spirit that I've experienced through embracing Existential Kink. And wealth. Did I mention wealth? I want you to have lots of genuine wealth. And romance. And community. All the "good stuff" in life.

In order to transmit to you the state of awareness that is Existential Kink, I'm going to need to take you down some immensely strange corridors of the psyche. I humbly ask that you pay close attention to the stories and anecdotes that I have to share with you from my own life and from the lives of my clients as they help bring this work to life.

I promise you, every moment of attention that you give to this book will be amply and exponentially rewarded by transformation in your own life.

Existential Kink has the power to vastly transform your life for *the way-better*, perhaps more than any other information that you will ever encounter.

Many of my clients have doubled or tripled their incomes, found the true loves of their lives, rejuvenated marriages worn out by resentment, healed chronic health conditions, discovered a deep sense of comfort in their own skins, and broken through ancient creative blocks. And I'll be sharing excerpts from their real-life stories of transformation throughout this book.

Sound a bit too good to be true?

Well, stick with me kid, 'cause I'm about to greatly expand your definition of how good "true" can be.

You see, what I'll be sharing with you here is Existential Kink, a radical, somatic, hot, and *eminently practical & quick* method of coming to love the previously hidden and shamed parts of your own self, so that your old negative patterns dissolve.

Those hidden and shamed parts? That's your shadow. And in the course of this book, you'll meet your shadow and learn how to dance with it.

When you do this work, when you integrate your shadow, you become much more capable of receiving big beauty and big bounty in your life because you're no longer accidentally, unknowingly rejecting it.

This is magic.

The magical worldview is this: As above, so below. As within, so without.

This means: reality is fractal and holographic. Tiny changes that you make within yourself can have dramatic effects in the "external" world because you and the "external" world are not truly separate. In other words, magic is possible *because* of the fractal and holographic nature of reality. When you change something "small" within yourself or your immediate environment, you automatically change something very "large"—the whole world.

This means that we are never *not* doing magic. We are always doing magic, we are always exerting influence. It's just that habitually, humans tend to do magic that's either just plain boring or destructive (there's that shadow again).

But the world is not separate from your psyche. They're part of one solid continuum, one solid weaving. Mastering practical magic involves learning what changes in yourself and your environment correspond to changes in the "outer" world of your experience.

Existential Kink has such transformative power because it deals with the integration of the conscious and the unconscious minds, in a cutting-edge, rapid way.

Why does integrating the conscious and the unconscious minds matter so much?

Because, as the pioneering psychotherapist Carl Jung (who was building on the insights of his mentor, Sigmund Freud) discovered, our conscious minds and identities (that is, the people we usually *imagine* ourselves to be) are just the very tippy tiny top of the immense underwater icebergs of our actual psychic totalities.

And oh, what giant, gnarly icebergs we all are!

The basic formula for profound alchemical change is *solve et coagula*, which means: to first utterly dissolve (*solve*) an existing form and then to carefully bring the dissolved and purified elements together again (*coagula*) in a whole new, more potent and finely organized, permutation.

Caterpillars, which completely dissolve wholly into goo inside their cocoons and then re-coagulate themselves into butterflies, provide a fantastic example of how this kind of alchemical change happens in nature. The English word *psyche*, meaning "soul" or "mind," comes from the Greek word *psyche*, meaning butterfly. Coincidence? I suspect not. Human souls, like butterflies, start out as wormy incipient forms that need to be dissolved and re-formed before our full glory can emerge.

Many self-help and popular magic books (for example, Law of Attraction stuff) focus heavily on the *coagula* phase of the *solve et coagula* formula.

Visualizing, praying, affirming, spell-casting, making vision board collages, creating sigils, charging crystals, doing loving-kindness meditation . . . all of these are well-known, time-tested, and effective means of *coagulating* ("manifesting" as it were) a new reality into existence. The only hitch is that the brighter we turn up the lights, the darker the shadows become.

All of the aforementioned popular "vibration raising" practices have a way of brightening the light in our being, which tends to intensify and sharpen the presence of our latent darkness.

So if one has not done *solve* processes on the underlying unconscious shadow patterns, desires, qualities, and beliefs that created sucky situations in your life to begin with—then all the visualizing and affirming in the world can only bring you shells of outwardly changed circumstances, *sans* genuinely satisfying fulfillment.

Perhaps this shallowness has been your experience, as it was mine, with your previous attempts at "manifestation." If one has not done sufficient *solve*, one is likely to become frustrated and lose enthusiasm (if one is anything like me) for magic and manifestation when results do not turn out as hoped.

Existential Kink will bring you in touch with the *solve* part of the equation: the dissolving, the uncovering, and ultimately, the embracing of your kinky-ass shadow.

What is *your* existential kink?

Have you met your shadow?

You see, when a person does not know how to become conscious of their own vast unconscious (and most people haven't the faintest idea of how to do this), they tend to be *controlled* by it, meaning their lives are dominated and limited by stubborn and painful patterns kept in motion by their disowned unconscious desires . . . which is something that no amount of visualizing or affirming can fix.

As Jung emphasized: "Until you make the unconscious, conscious, it will rule your life and you will call it Fate."

But Jung also pointed out: "One does not become enlightened by *imagining* figures of light, but by making the darkness conscious."

That's exactly what this here lil' self-help book is all about: we're not here to imagine figures of light; we're here to make the darkness conscious, in a fun, fast, and kinky way.

The Unconscious

J ung's observation that "Until you make the unconscious, conscious, it will rule your life and you will call it Fate" means that
your unconscious desires and curiosities have great power to
shape your experience.

It's tricky: After all, these deep shadowy desires and curiosities of yours are unknown and *unconscious* (meaning: you are
not *knowingly* aware of them, so they do not seem like they are
yours at all!). Yet these taboo, disowned, and repressed desires do
tend to get fulfilled in your life. When this happens, *because* these
taboo desires of yours have been disowned and repressed, you
won't recognize their fulfillments *as* fulfillments. Instead these
fulfillments of your deepest desires will often seem to your conscious mind like awful calamities. Thus it tends to seem like some
agency outside of you—some call it cruel Fate—is making bad
stuff happen to poor lil' ole you.

Consider the case of a young man in his twenties, Alex, who
has a deep desire to experience himself as "taken care of." Maybe
he never got to fully experience himself as taken care of as a little
child, so the unmet need is still within him. But Alex's desire isn't
socially acceptable for a man his age.

Thus, the desire to be dependent and "taken care of" is taboo
and so it gets repressed into his unconscious. It's so far outside
his awareness that he doesn't even *know* that this desire is within
him, and he very well might not believe you if you told him.

Alex consciously desires what he's been told he "should"
want: that is to be independent and autonomous and have a cool
career. So Alex visualizes and affirms success, works on being

upbeat and "high-vibe" and he gets a hip, respectable job after he graduates college. But in a few months, despite Alex's best intentions, his unconscious gets the better of him and he "accidentally" gets fired from the job. Now he can't pay rent on his own, and so he has to go live with his parents again.

To his conscious mind, this feels to him like a huge failure, humiliation, and calamity.

To his unconscious, this is a giant victory and a great fulfillment of the deep underlying desire—*his desire to want to be taken care of.*

Unconsciously, Alex is enjoying living with his parents and being taken care of. The ironic thing is: as long as Alex resists allowing himself to consciously experience his job loss and his being "taken care of" by his parents as a great victory and fulfillment (in other words, as long as he resists *consenting* to experience it as kinkily awesome *the very same way his unconscious experiences it*), then the more he will feel out-of-control and cursed by Fate.

As long as Alex refuses to consciously enjoy his circumstance, he'll be inclined to see himself as a loser and a failure, he'll lose confidence, and he'll stay stuck.

Paradoxically, the moment Alex becomes willing to "get on the side" of his taboo unconscious desire for dependence and goes ahead and deeply savors its victory—at that moment he can feel empowered again. He can realize that his taboo wish to be dependent has been fulfilled, and let himself receive the hot weird pleasure of that.

Then, rather than being a loser, Alex is actually a massively fulfilled person. From this vantage point of deciding to consciously allow himself to enjoy and be satisfied by his previously unconscious pleasure, it's then much easier for him to go ahead and make his way in the world. In essence, he's no longer guilty;

he's not beating himself up anymore. He's no longer resisting his situation, so it doesn't need to persist.

This young man's enjoyment of his "failure" and "dependence" and state of "being taken care of" might seem perverse, weird.

And indeed, of course, it is.

Yet it's precisely in this perverse, weird, and shameless enjoyment of his sucky situation that the transformation of his life and the liberation of his energies lie. Alex has taken the dark and heretofore unconscious pleasure of his shadow and brought it into the light.

There are many, many such unconscious patterns that affect our tender caterpillar lives, but here's a handy list of several common examples. See if you can recognize any of these patterns from your own life or from the lives of your friends and family members:

- Only being able to earn a certain amount of money each month, no matter how hard or how much you work

- Only being attracted to partners who turn out to bear an uncanny resemblance to your asshole dad (or to your asshole mom, or to the first person who broke your heart, or whatever)

- Hearing the mean voice of your third-grade teacher in your head whenever you sit down to create, so you avoid creating

- Overeating (or overindulging in drugs, alcohol, etc.) to cover up feelings of guilt, shame, loneliness, frustration that seem endless

- Disliking yourself/your body no matter what your shape

- Perpetually feeling victimized and like your life would be good if only rude other people (your family, your boss, your spouse, your employees, the government, the blacks, the gays, the straights, the whites, the Jews, the Christians, the capitalists, the hippies, etc., etc.) would stop messing with you

- Having grand plans for the future, but never getting around to taking the first concrete steps to realizing those plans

- Being very sensitive and taking everything personally

- Habitually seeking approval, doing things to get people to like you even when you don't really want to do those things

- Picking a fight with your partner just when everything starts getting really good

You get the idea.

None of these patterns are original in the least. Literally billions of us humans suffer from them. They're all passed down from family and culture, the delectable inheritances of trauma, guilt, and shame. They're very, *very* repetitive and predictable.

Most all of us have at least a few of these patterns in operation, and most people never manage to shift their sticky patterns at all. The majority of folks aren't even *willing to acknowledge* that they're in the grips of a pattern and therefore are not truly in control of their own lives—indeed, such an idea is very threatening to the ordinary ego.

If you doubt this, just think of how many people you know who are stuck in relationships or careers or mindsets that aren't working. From the outside, you can see that if only they took a few simple steps they could change their whole world, but they don't take those steps—they *won't* take those steps. Why? They're being ruled by their unconscious, and the foul scenes that they themselves are creating and perpetuating just seem to them to be their unwelcome Fate.

Dissolving unconscious patterns by making them conscious (and thereby integrating your being, your will) allows you to wake up out of this powerlessness and become the captain of the ship of your own life.

Once you do this kind of *solve* work on your unconscious, then the well-known methods of visualization, affirmation, spell-casting, and so forth, work quite beautifully, and with far less frustration.

Up to now this kind of waking up has been a relatively rare feat among us humans. Some individuals have achieved it through decades of psychotherapy, and some have done it through a similarly long period of sitting meditation.

What this book proposes is a different method—the "EK" method—a method for *rapidly* making the unconscious, conscious—so that your unconscious desires and curiosities no longer rule you. When that happens, a huge vista of possibility opens up in your life.

This method of integration works within days, weeks, and months rather than within years and decades. Why? Because Existential Kink doesn't just identify your shadow self. Existential Kink teaches you to *embrace and love* your shadow self.

Consider: the unconscious rules not only our night-time dreams, but to a great extent (a far, far greater extent than is comfortable for us to acknowledge)—it also rules the patterns, desires, and curiosities that shape our waking experience.

Our day-to-day waking experience is also a kind of dream—more dense and more slow-moving than our nighttime dreams, yes, but still a dream nonetheless.

When we know how to consciously, deliberately work with the contents of the unconscious, we gain an amazing degree of control over our waking lives—just as a lucid dreamer gains remarkable control over their night-time dreams by first becoming conscious that they are asleep and dreaming.

This work of becoming profoundly, skillfully lucid and empowered in the dream of daily waking life is what I have to share with you here.

Once you stop feeling alienated, as "other" from your shadow, you will start feeling powerful.

This book presents a life-altering shadow integration meditative practice that invites us to make conscious the unconscious pleasure that we take in the stuck, painful patterns of our lives. Through consciously enjoying and giving approval to these previously unconscious "guilty pleasures," we interrupt and end the stuck patterns so that we can get what we really want in our lives.

I should mention that Existential Kink, while fresh, is not entirely without precedent. Throughout all schools of tantric gnosticism (Hindu, Buddhist, and in the Western Esoteric tradition), there's an emphasis on learning how to stay present in high sensation. By "high sensation" I mean both intense physical feelings like pain and pleasure—and also intense emotional feelings, like anger, fear, and lust.

Tantrikas therefore traditionally meditate on intensely charged subject matter like sex and death, and focus on learning how to transmute the raw energies of emotion and instinct (especially sex and aggression) into the luminosity of free awareness.

The fundamental tantric idea is that it's important to *work with* the strong energies of attraction and aversion, pleasure and pain, to facilitate awakening, rather than avoiding them. Why? Because avoiding desire, aggression, and socially taboo experience doesn't help; avoidance only deepens the trap of aversion and attachment, which causes the wheel of illusion to keep spinning.

Likewise, in Existential Kink we focus on delving into taboo territories of our unconscious minds and learn to stay present with the high sensation there, in a way that transmutes the previously-stuck energy into free awareness.

Lesson 1
Super-Freak Divine Alchemy

(On How God Is One Kinky-Ass Motherfucker,
and the Magical Implications Thereof)

This lesson includes:

- Godself Kink

- The Great Work

- The Vast Self

- Making Your Fate

- On Spell-casting

- A Basic Concept

- The Spirit

- The Sexual Process of Magic

Godself Kink

Let's return to a point mentioned in the Introduction: if the ancient wisdom of Vedas are correct and the whole universe is just God playing elaborate rounds of hide'n'seek with Godself, then God is a super-freak.

We need only look around our planet to see that God's idea of a fun time includes some seriously edgy, ultra-taboo, hardcore stuff—including war and poverty and pain and ravaging and abuse and atrocities of all variety.

That's a whole lot of sadism and masochism, dominance and submission, bondage and torture—in both extreme and subtle forms—that God enjoys playing out with Godself.

I propose that all our suffering and stuckness in life comes from forgetting that we're divine sparks playing a wild kinky game and that great miracles can come forth in our lives when we reverse the process of forgetting by deliberately reclaiming the pleasure of the game—not just in our minds, but in our hearts and genitals.

I acknowledge this might be difficult to accept, especially after two thousand years of Christianity insisting on a God that's wholly "good" (who, nonetheless, is constantly, mysteriously counterbalanced by a powerful evil Devil).

But it simply stands to reason that if we want to consciously embody our *whole* divine inheritance and become true magicians, to become people who are capable of attaining our most meaningful aims and experiencing bountiful fulfillment, healing, and love in our daily lives, then we need to wake ourselves up in the midst of this great freaky game, by savoring it, enjoying it, grieving exquisitely for it, getting off on it . . . just like God does.

When we do this, we become lucid in the dream of waking life, capable of executing marvels. We become undeniably, tangibly aware of the divine presence, the spark of Godself within us.

We start to perceive our lives from the perspective of the divine curiosity within us, instead of from our grasping egos.

Our inner divinity ceases to be a sweet, comforting New Age idea and instead becomes a tangible, electrifying, *felt* reality. When we do this work, we put into concrete application the famous alchemical dictum from the Emerald Tablet: "As above, so below; as within, so without." It's easy to give lip service to that dramatic notion of cosmic correspondence which is at the heart of a magical worldview, but it's a whole other thing to actually *live* it. This "living it" bit is the essence of Existential Kink.

Consider this: our conscious selves (the selves who we usually take ourselves to be) definitely *do not* want all the "bad stuff" of life. In other words, our conscious selves (otherwise known as "egos") believe that instead of failure, humiliation, poverty, illness, rejection, and sadness, we would much rather have wins, success, wealth, health, romance, joy, and so forth. But as the Buddha observed, "All sentient beings want to be happy; and all sentient beings suffer." In other words, it seems that in life we often end up getting *the opposite* of what we say we want. And, as Hollywood celebrities well know, it's possible to "have everything"—all the good stuff of the world, and still be totally, pathetically, wildly miserable.

So what gives? Clearly something nasty is going on here.

I'd offer the following explanation: as humans, our whole selves are always reflections of the divine totality ("As above, so below; as within, so without"). We are microcosmic reflections of the total holy macrocosm, and as such, we are each innately curious about and *desirous for* the full spectrum of potential experience, both the painful and the pleasurable, the evil and the good, the ugly and the beautiful.

Really let this sink in for a minute.

And contrary to some airy Law of Attraction notions, we rarely get what we consciously want (unless we do the kind of deep *solve* work addressed in this book), but we always get what we *unconsciously* want.

And if you're curious as to what you *unconsciously* want, you don't need thirty years of psychoanalysis to figure it out: you can just take a look at what you currently have in your life and know that that's exactly what your unconscious wants, because what your unconscious wants, *it gets*. This is something we'll discuss more in a bit.

As long as we insist that we absolutely *don't* want dark, freaky, *unpleasant* things, a major part of our full-spectrum human curiosity gets cut off, repressed, denied, and made unconscious. And this is *bad news bears*, because desire-curiosities in the unconscious have much, *much* more power to become manifest in material reality than our conscious, "good," ego-approved desires do.

We need to learn how to own up to the darker side of our human curiosity and take such deep, shameless responsibility for it, and admit that we are willing to enjoy its challenging manifestations. If we do not own up, then we are likely to stay stuck in the same cycle of unconscious creation of scary stuff. Let's pause and consider the relation of what we're talking about to another, very grand idea—the Great Work of Alchemy.

The Great Work

The work of becoming a magical force of nature is very much connected to what the alchemists called the Great Work. Now don't get too alarmed when I tell you this, but the process of the Great Work is identical to the process of enlightenment (also known as individuation, awakening, initiation, or "becoming whole"). In short, it's the process of coming to viscerally identify less as a sorry, isolated individual and more and more as a wave in the ocean of God. While this is a very lofty endeavor, the pursuit of it also yields many tangible rewards.

As we grow in the Great Work, our consciousness evolves and integrates, and when our consciousness changes in this way, we become much more capable of seeing and acting upon beautiful worldly opportunities for fulfillment.

Indeed, for myself I've found in this process there's often a repeated fairy tale sense of "veils being lifted" and the realization that what I wanted was "there all along" for the taking. I just was too blind or dull to notice it before.

The first major stage of the Great Work was known to alchemists as the *unio mentalis*, the creation of a unified mind.

It's important to note that "mind" in this alchemical sense does not just mean the ordinary thinking mind: it means unity within *your own being*, your thoughts, your emotion, and your will. We might say it's more like a "unified mentality" or "unified attitude." The symbol of the *unio mentalis* would be a high-powered, whole heart.

The *unio mentalis* is a being that is not in conflict with itself; it's undivided and thus is extremely powerful. The *unio mentalis* phase of the Great Work is what we're dealing with here in this book.

It's important to note that the *unio mentalis* isn't just nice to have for mystical reasons—it's also highly pragmatic. The *unio mentalis* is synonymous with having "a united will," what ancient Greek thaumaturgists considered the absolute precondition to effective practical magic, or, in other words, the deliberate generation of positive synchronous experiences.

The second major stage of the Great Work was called the *unus mundus*, or "one world," and it's an expansion of unity. It's the condition of your soul-spirit being so seamlessly incarnate and at one with the world that you can do things like walk on water, or turn into a rainbow of light when you die, leaving behind only your hair and fingernails.

I'm still working on figuring that bit out.

But even though the *unio mentalis* isn't as grand as spontaneously combusting into a giant rainbow or literally turning water into wine, it still brings you *much* further along in the process of the Great Work than most people will ever go. Plus, achieving the *unio mentalis* tends to be a precondition for figuring out how to get to the *unus mundus*. In other words, unless you're united within your own heart-mind, you're unlikely to find the path to embodied unity with all reality.

In the Western Esoteric tradition popularized in the twentieth century by the Golden Dawn and Aleister Crowley, reaching the *unio mentalis* corresponds to something called "gaining the Knowledge and Conversation of the Holy Guardian Angel" or the K&C of the HGA for short. It's important to note that while the Holy Guardian Angel is often experienced as a distinct, autonomous "person"—as an "Other" within the psyche, like the Anima/Animus—it's also often met as an intuitive understanding of profound, nonlocal, and nonlinear connection.

This first *unio mentalis* stage of the Great Work that we're concerned with here involves healing the disconnect between our ideals, intentions, and inspirations (our spirit, the "masculine" or "projective" part of our being) and our embodied, emotional, sexual, creative energy (our soul, the "feminine" or "receptive" part of us, which is also the part of us that gets fertilized and "gives birth" to synchronous experiences in the outer world).

Why does this matter?

Because most of us are walking around with terribly divided wills, and thus a weakened ability to fulfill our true potential.

The Vast Self

Consider this: on a soul-spirit level we're each grand cosmic hermaphrodites, endlessly self-fertilizing. Our spirit and our soul are both elements of the larger divine Self that we are. The higher Self that we are is unconscious in most human beings and so, as we've mentioned, it speaks mostly in dreams and through the manifestation of events (i.e. "synchronicities").

When you begin to experience communications from the total Self not solely through dreams and synchronicities but as direct "knowing" within your own waking awareness, that's called the Knowledge and Conversation of the Holy Guardian Angel in the Western Esoteric tradition, which is also known as relating consciously to your inner Other (Anima/Animus), a process which Jung referred to as "the masterwork of individuation."

We could venture to guess that the vast Self is unconscious in most modern human beings because we all seem to have a strong interest in experiencing ourselves as separate, alienated egos, little isolated particles who exist at the mercy of cruel fate and outside circumstance. Think about it: if the Self contains *everything*, then the way to experience yourself as separate is to identify yourself with only one side of a polarity and to disdain the other side, to pretend it's "*soooooooo* not you."

Voila! As soon as you've done this creative pretending, you've (temporarily, fictionally) created an ego self that's apparently separate from the whole Self. To maintain this fictional sense of separation, the ego-personality that we take ourselves to be harshly judges, disowns, and denies *huuuuuuge* parts of our actual being, thus rendering them "unconscious" and creating the personal and collective shadow.

We refer to this work as "shadow integration," but it's also just "Self integration." The Self includes *all* archetypes, all gods and daimons. Integrating the "naughty stuff" in what we call the shadow is just one part of relating to the previously unconscious Self, which includes the *whole* of our unconscious divinity.

Making Your Fate

Let's revisit that incredibly important observation by Carl Jung that I mentioned earlier:

"Until you make your unconscious, conscious, it will rule your life and you will call it Fate."

In other words, the emotions and desires and positions that our ego disowns inevitably haunt us (personally and collectively) by generating painful synchronous experiences that urge us to confront and reintegrate the disdained side of a polarity. This is what Jung's predecessor, Sigmund Freud, called "the return of the repressed."

Polarities include all sets of "opposites"—masculine and feminine, fire and ice, night and day, violence and healing, creation and destruction, good and evil, fulfillment and deprivation, power and powerlessness, etc.

Let me give you an example: most of us have grown up in a society that exalts wealth, and we have disowned and denied the other side of the polarity: a love of scarcity. In doing so we make our love of scarcity unconscious, and thus scarcity synchronously shows up in our lives, until we agree to consciously, deliberately, "insanely," shamelessly love it.

The Great Work involves making the unconscious, conscious and thus changing the locus of our agency and taking charge of our own fate.

To change the locus of your agency means to stop aligning yourself with your ego's one-sided choices (the ego tends to want only what it labels "the good stuff") and to instead align yourself with the kinkier, more adventurous choices of the underlying total divine presence that we all are: the strange, vast Self which enjoys and is very curious about *absolutely everything.*

To do this, we have to greatly humble our ego's denial and fictional (if we were feeling feisty we might even say *delusional)* sorting of all experience into "good" (what appears to benefit me) and "bad" (what appears to *not* benefit me). When we succeed in this, the ego loses layers of its absorption in the fiction of separation, and comes more and more to see itself as just a particular (rather funny) expression of a much larger divine whole, the Self.

The Self with a capital "S" is the primal Selfhood of everything and everyone, which is (paradoxically) also our own real inner selfhood. This is so because the Self is infinite consciousness. It's as if all of us humans are light bulbs, and the Self is the electricity that powers us. In becoming more identified with this underlying whole that we share with everyone, we paradoxically become more uniquely individual because we become free of our attachment to conventional, socially prescribed roles.

In waking up out of our absorbing fiction of separation, we link up the gigantic sexual, taboo, electrical energy (the shakti, the turn-on) in our bodies with our most inspired ideals and intentions. Then our ideals and our intentions gain the high-voltage electric "oomph" that they've been previously missing.

The more you fulfill the Great Work, the better you get at actual, material manifestation in the world.

The Basque word for witch, *sorginak,* means "one who makes her own fate." What I'm presenting to you here is a way to make your own fate: a witchy, tricksy, feminine path to enlightenment that's quite a bit different than the more publicly vaunted, masculine routes of asceticism, contemplation, and yogic saintliness.

The witchy path of the Great Work involves learning to get off on (and thus to tangibly, viscerally reintegrate) the darkest, scariest dimensions of ourselves and our existence. It's a sexual, worldly, orgasmic, ecstatic path which bears a good deal in common with Hindu and Buddhist tantric traditions. To be completely blunt, this Existential Kink work is the left-hand path. The left-hand path is also known as "the lightning path" because it wakes you up very quickly (quick as lightning) and it destroys who you think you are (lightning torches what it hits).

Sounds exciting, yes?

On Spell-casting

To cast a spell is to communicate with your personal unconscious and the collective unconscious in a way that generates specific results through synchronicity. Believe it or not, you are casting spells at every single moment. Your words, your actions, the looks you give yourself in the mirror and the looks you give to other people. Your clothes. Your perfume. Your songs. Your smiles. Your laughter. Your reactivity and resentment. All spells.

You constantly communicate with your own individual unconscious and with the collective unconscious. You constantly perform who you believe yourself to be, as well as projecting the social identity and conditioning that you have imbibed. And since your performance of your identity entails a perpetual communication with your unconscious and the collective unconscious, you perpetually generate circumstances, relationships, and synchronicities that mirror and affirm and elaborate your identification.

If you want to know who you unconsciously believe you are, just take a look at your life, your surroundings, your relationship. Your life mirrors those deep beliefs.

The circumstances and relationships that we create often just don't feel "synchronous" or "magical" because they're repetitions that we're accustomed to; they feel maybe a bit boring and confining, a bit expected. Many of us have unconsciously accepted conditioned identities as "wrong" or "broken" or

"deserving of resentment" or "not deserving to be highly valued"—and so we continue to magically generate results that
reflect and affirm that.

I can't emphasize enough that this does not mean you are
to "blame" for difficult circumstances and relationships that your
unconscious creates. You, as an individual, are not "to blame" or
culpable for karmic or social conditioning created beyond your
individual, conscious choice.

You are, however, as an individual, *the only person* capable of
altering your unconscious conditioning and identity, and restoring
it to its divine reality. You are *capable*; you are not "at fault" or "to
blame."

A Basic Concept

I'm going to make explicit a concept that I will probably repeat
many times, because it's key to this work. Please learn it.

The concept is this: You are not who you think you are.

Whoever you happen to think you are, I assure you, you are
not that. I suggest that you remind yourself of this often, because
it makes this work easier.

When you brush your teeth in the morning, think to yourself,
"I'm not at all who I imagine myself to be. I'm something entirely
different and far more vast and strange. Hmmmm. I wonder what
I really am?"

Who you think you are is largely a societally constructed fiction held together by some compulsively repetitive thoughts and
stories, and it bears little or no resemblance to the being that you
actually are. As the wise and pithy magician Mr. Lon Milo Duquette
says: "Magic is indeed all in your head, but your head is a hell of a
lot bigger than you think it is." In other words, the whole "external"
world is actually "within" consciousness. No one has ever experienced an "objective" world outside of their subjective awareness.

Even the most rigorous scientific experiment can only be experienced subjectively. There's simply no world outside of our subjective awareness.

The Spirit

The spirit is the active, projective part of the Self that perceives perfection, and it broadcasts inspirations based on its perception of endless possibility and perfection.

Our ego-personality, our conscious mind, often mistranslates these inspirations into a lot of opinions about how things "should" be, which maintains our sense of alienation.

These opinions tend to have a kind of imperative force to them, such as:

"People should be kinder."

"I should get in shape and eat more greens."

"The world should be fair."

"We shouldn't have to use money; everything should be a gift economy."

"I should only want to have sex with appropriate people."

On and on and on and on, forever.

Remember, the spirit sees no limits, only pure simultaneous infinity and possibility. And when the conscious ego mind picks up on impressions from the spirit, it struggles to translate those into this limited material world, so those impressions of infinity end up sounding like ideas about how things "should be." And the spirit-as-translated-by-the-ego, with all its infinity and opinions, tends to be quite judgmental of the animal self, with all its messy excretions and sexual desires and messy kitchens and appetites for cheesecake.

But the weird thing is, behind all this "should" stuff and all these judgments and opinions, there's this magnificent power that the spirit has.

This magnificent power usually goes untapped in a human life.

You see, the super-power of the spirit is total approval, total embrace, total celebration, the total perception of the already-existing perfection of life. When the spirit exclaims "perfect!" the conscious mind/the ego tends to hear that as "make things more perfect! They suck now!"—but actually what the spirit is saying is "everything is perfect right now!"

Yes, everything. The world and our selves in all their fucked-up glory.

That experience of total approval and total embrace, total absence of shame or aversion, is what the spirit is always trying to teach us about and it's ironically what our conscious mind mistranslates as all those "shoulds" and judgments.

Okay, so how do we change this state of affairs?

The Sexual Process of Magic

Existential Kink is a potent form of magic (also known as: "psychological integration") in which the receptive feminine—the unconscious, the disowned and denied, the soul—becomes pregnant with the perfection-vision of our spirit—the masculine, projective part of our being, and eventually gives birth to positive synchronous manifestations in our lives.

This is actually the esoteric meaning of the Immaculate Conception. The Virgin Mary becomes pregnant with the total approval spirit energy of God—she lets its energy flow all the way down through her, to her instinctual animal self and genitals. When she does that, she conceives and later gives birth to Jesus Christ, who is a symbol of the *Anima Mundi*, the World Soul, aka the Self.

Okay, so that's some far-out metaphysical stuff, what the hell does that mean, in practical terms?

What that means is you're going to take all the embracing-approval-seeking-inherent-perfection-perceiving power of your spirit, tell your ego "thanks but you can shut the fuck up for a while," and send all that embracing-approval-seeking-inherent-perfection-perceiving down to your actual life, body, emotions, and present situation.

In the process of Existential Kink you invite your spirit to have the realization that your life on earth—right now, right here, in this animal, human body—is actually exactly what it has always wanted to celebrate with its exultant songs of perfection.

Another way of saying that is that the practice of Existential Kink is the work of becoming attuned to practical magic; you decide to fully incarnate, to agree fully to be who you already are, however messy or stinky that may be—with no reservation, no hold-back, no "if-only," no judgment, no shame.

And in dropping your resistance and negative judgment, you bring yourself fully into resonance with practical reality, which happens to be the only position from which you can effectively influence it.

Most of us human beings have spirits-that-are-poorly-translated-by-egos into lots of judgment and stand-offish-ness—most have us have conscious minds that have not yet fully committed to incarnation, and that's why we're not unstoppable forces of nature.

When you fully commit to incarnation here, in this material plane, fully commit to being who-you-already-are-and-having-the-experience-you're-already-having with total orgasmic kinky joy—there's a paradox right there.

The paradox is that once you fully commit to being who you already are, having what you already have, and hugely celebrating it, you become a masterful practical magician, a force of nature capable of shifting circumstances very easily.

Your degree of success in becoming lucid in this waking dream of the earth corresponds precisely to your willingness to have your ego step aside and allow your spirit to drench your animal self, your unconscious, and all your actual circumstances, with its high-powered perception of utter perfection.

When you do this, to speak in sexy terms, your spirit is able to plant the loving seed of "already totally perfect! Wow!" in the womb of your unconscious, creative self. Then, magically speaking, what happens is that seed of "already totally perfect! Wow!" gestates in the womb of your unconscious self, and in a matter of days or weeks or months, eventually your unconscious self births the child of that seed into the world . . . in the form of circumstances, new awareness, synchronicities, people, events.

In this metaphor, the child of the perception-of-perfection, the child sired by the approving wisdom of your spirit unmediated by the delusional ego, is your magical result, your positive synchronicity.

You see, the unconscious, creative, animal part of us is always getting impregnated with seeds from the spirit and is always giving birth to magical results. But usually those seeds from the spirit have been genetically modified by the ego, which, as we discussed, takes the "perfection!" impulse of the spirit and perpetually mistranslates it as "this should be perfect, but it isn't! This Sucks! Why isn't it perfect yet? This is all wrong! This is terrible; I hate this!"

So what usually happens is that the creative, receptive part of us (the unconscious) gets pregnant with these seeds of refusal, shaming, judgment, rejection. And then she gives birth to magical results—to circumstances and experiences and synchronicities and relationships in our lives—that have this quality of stimulating feelings of shame and refusal and rejection in us.

To use dualistic language, we might say that before we get very deliberate about this work, we often create "negative" synchronicities. In other words, synchronicities or "meaningful coincidences" are perpetually happening: there's always a perfect, poetic rhyming mirror relationship between who you most deeply know yourself to be and what you externally experience.

Sadly, it's just that most people deeply (unconsciously) believe themselves and the world to be wrong and "not good enough," so they experience external synchronicities in their lives that rhyme with and affirm "wrong" and "not good enough."

The practice of Existential Kink that I'm about to share with you is a rapid and effective means of turning around who you most deeply experience yourself to be, thereby greatly improving the quality of synchronous experience in your life.

Lesson 2
The Seven Axioms of Existential Kink

This lesson includes:

- Having is evidence of wanting

- We have a choice as to whether we experience sensation as pleasure or pain

- It's possible to get off on every "stroke," and every happening in life is a "stroke"

- The degree of being "turned off" or "turned on" is a factor of approval

- Desire evolves through fulfillment, not denial and repression

- Shame is the Magic Killer

- The truth is sensational

An axiom is a proposition that's assumed without proof for the sake of studying the consequences that follow. In other words, the seven axioms I'll present are working propositions that I can't "prove" to you are true, but I *can* say that if you experiment with accepting them as true and see what consequences result from that acceptance, you will find those results to be fascinating and rewarding.

1) *Having is evidence of wanting*

This axiom can be a bit of a shocking and uncomfortable idea, especially if you've had hardships in your life in the past or present. It can be very jarring to consider those as something that you "wanted." But, again, it's not the conscious part of us that "wants" difficulties or negative patterns. It's the *unconscious* part of us. The daemonic part. The part of us that we don't usually identify with, but that nevertheless strongly impacts our experience.

"Having is evidence of wanting" is another way of phrasing the pithy quote that we previously read from the old wizard Carl Jung: "Until you make the unconscious conscious, it will direct your life and you will call it Fate." Jung explained throughout his work that your unconscious is the fertile, receptive, magically efficacious part of you. The unconscious is generative because the emotions, symbols, and attitudes within it create the synchronicities, or meaningful coincidences, that shape your experience. Whatever desires are in your unconscious, will be "born," *will* happen, and the results of those desires will seem to be come toward you from some unfathomable outside agency—in other words, "fate."

The good news is, when you do the uncomfortable work of making these strong, unconscious desire-curiosities conscious, by giving them a vast, taboo-level of approval, they lose their fateful power to fuck with you.

So the purpose of the axiom "having is evidence of wanting" is not at all to blame anyone or to shame them for their experience ("you're so horrible! you wanted this!")—as shame and blame are highly, highly counterproductive in integration work (as the more you shame something the more unconscious it will become!)—but rather the purpose of the axiom is to serve as an *excavation tool*, so that you can gently and humorously begin digging for the unconscious desire-curiosities that shape your experience, and in that way become massively empowered to own those desires with a deep sense of sovereignty and agency and to thereby positively change our experience.

Because most of us human beings have many "negative" unconscious desires, when most beginning magicians try their hands at "manifestation," they may think it "doesn't work" because we don't get what our conscious mind wants, or because we get something that resembles what we thought we wanted, but it turns out to kind of suck.

That's the sort of big bummer that can be very confusing, and that causes many would-be magicians to just give up and decide it's all a bunch of nonsense.

But here's the kicker: even the most amateur form of magic or half-assed attempt at fulfilling a goal always works perfectly to bring us what our being actually, most deeply wants—that is, what our *unconscious* wants. And since we're always doing magic "accidentally" all the time anyways, it's an excellent idea to do magic deliberately, so you can become more aware and in control of the process of desiring and receiving.

So I invite you to consider the idea that any current situations in your life, especially those situations that tend to recur over and over again in an annoying pattern (i.e., you can only seem to bring in a certain amount of money each month, you can only seem to attract the same kind of less-than-awesome partner, you feel repeatedly betrayed by friends, etc.), are the result of your already-always-happening accidental magic, and as such they represent a beautiful fulfillment of a deep desire in your unconscious.

Naturally when I mention that "having is evidence of wanting," folks are quick to bring up children stuck in devastated war zones or abusive situations and say, "How can you say they wanted that? What kind of horrible monster would dare suggest such a thing?"

Well, to this I say: first of all, it's not just our personal unconscious desires that affect the external situations in anyone's life— it's the collective unconscious desires.

Here's a rule of thumb: If we're talking about an annoying pattern that seems to recur specifically for you, and you know a lot of other folks who are free of that particular pattern, chances are good that it's something that's being created specifically by your own personal unconscious. But if we're talking about endemic human problems like war or racism or child abuse, odds are it's more of a collective unconscious issue.

So war and abuse and all the challenging stuff that transpires in the world result from millennia of un-integrated, repressed, denied shadow desires of individuals conglomerated into collective forces.

Second of all, I don't think it's enormously far-fetched to imagine that some very brave and generous souls come into this world with the strong personal, unconscious desire to experience extreme hardships in childhood, perhaps for the ultimate purpose of making it conscious and healing it, and in that way, healing the collective.

Third of all, even a child or person in a terrible situation generated by the collective can improve their situation through taking a magically efficacious approach to it. The attitudes of self-pity, hopelessness, resentment, bitterness, while very understandable and also fun and satisfying to indulge in sometimes, are, alas, not magically efficacious in creating happy synchronicities and outcomes.

Finally, the most surefire way to help address the collective shadow is to do the work to become aware of and to integrate your own personal unconscious desires, and to help others (who express a sincere interest) to do the same. The brutal circumstances wrought by the collective are made up of unconscious individuals, so the more aware you personally become as an individual, the more you "clean up" your own influence on the collective.

2) We have a choice as to whether we experience sensation as pleasure or as pain

Many of us aren't used to deliberately exercising this choice, so we may not have even realized that we have it. But we do. Sensation is qualitatively neutral. It's our mind's interpretation of sensation that decides whether or not we experience it as "painful" or "pleasurable." As the poet John Milton observed in *Paradise Lost*, "The mind is its own place and in itself, can make a Heaven of Hell, a Hell of Heaven."

A simple example: I love brussels sprouts, and eating them is a pleasure for me. Some people hate the sulphorous taste of brussels sprouts, and experience eating them as a kind of pain.

A more extreme example: childbirth is a notoriously painful process, often depicted in modern media as filled with screams and groans and facilitated by numbing drugs. And yet there's something called the Orgasmic Birth movement, which consists of women who train themselves to experience the intense sensations of child birth as pleasure, and many women are indeed able to experience their births as an orgasm instead of a horrible painful ordeal.

That's not to say that it's *easy* to train oneself to experience the very intense sensations of childbirth as pleasurable, but just that it's *possible*. And the fact that it's *possible* points very directly to the immensely flexible capacity of the human organism to choose how it perceives sensation. Exercising choice over how you perceive the sensations of happenings in your life and psyche is a profound step in releasing attachment to being "helpless" and at the mercy of "cruel fate."

To point to the explicit analogy from which the notion of Existential Kink arises, in sexual kink, or BDSM, a lot of people around the world deliberately choose to engage in painful experiences—flogging, bondage, having hot wax dripped on them—and derive pleasure and satisfaction from those experiences.

It was in reflecting on this phenomenon of sexual kink/BDSM especially that Existential Kink was born. I started to wonder why it is that we don't usually experience the painful parts of life as similar playful pleasure.

I think it has to do with the matter of choice.

People participating in BDSM consciously *choose* to be tied up and flogged, and that element of deliberate choice allows them to experience that pain and bondage as a kind of play, as something fun. But usually when painful things happen in our lives, we don't feel that we have a "choice" whether or not to experience them as pain, so we don't find it very fun—instead we tend to experience it as very disempowering and defeating.

So a big part of Existential Kink involves deciding to at least start by "pretending" (i.e., experimentally accepting the axiom "having is evidence of wanting") that some hitherto-unconscious part of you playfully, humorously, curiously chooses and desires a given painful situation, behavior, stream of thought, or mood.

When you make a kinky game of it, you greatly expand your sense of agency, you unite your will, and you open up room for a sense of fun and playfulness to come into the scene.

3) It's possible to get off on every stroke—and every happening in life is a "stroke"

The notion of "getting off on every stroke" is something I learned while in the Orgasmic Meditation movement.

In Orgasmic Meditation, a "stroker" strokes a woman's clitoris very lightly for fifteen minutes, within a very specific container involving a timer, gloves, lube, and a "nest" of pillows and blankets. Orgasmic Meditation is a kind of very simplified, "Zen" sort of tantric practice (if you look up traditional Hindu or Buddhist Tantra you'll see they're quite complicated) where the goal is to focus on the sensation at the point of contact between finger and clitoris, much like the point of Vipassana meditation is to focus on the sensation at the point of the breath entering the nose.

If you're a woman being stroked in Orgasmic Meditation, you soon notice that there are certain kinds of clitoral strokes that you automatically prefer and enjoy, and some that don't feel as good, or even that feel a little uncomfortable or painful. So an advanced challenge in the Orgasmic Meditation practice is to attempt to open oneself to enjoy, to be turned on by, and "get off on" strokes that are outside one's automatic range of preference. In this way, one learns to expand one's experience of orgasmic (i.e., pleasure) energy (in Orgasmic Meditation, as in Existential Kink, the definition of "orgasm" or "getting off" is not limited to the convulsions of climax but extends to all pleasure), and thus to become more aware and awake in high sensation.

This practice of "getting off on every stroke" can, by analogy, be extended beyond the context of Orgasmic Meditation (or sex) and be applied to life, wherein one considers everything that happens as a "stroke." As in,

Comments that other people make to you—those are strokes.

Surprising situations that arise—those are strokes.

A critical monologue from some inner voice—those are strokes.

In any given day, there are all kinds of "strokes" that come towards us from other people, from our own minds, and from "fate." The more we're willing to "get off on every stroke" that comes to us, the more pleasure and fun we can have in our lives, and the more magnetic we can become to positive synchronicity.

Sadly, most of us turn ourselves off. We have a quite narrow range of "strokes" that we're willing to get off on in our day. Someone is super nice to us? Turn-on. We get a big unexpected gift of money? Turn-on. The sun is shining? Turn-on. Someone is rude to us? Turn-off. Grey, cold, drizzly day? Turn-off. Low bank account? Turn-off.

The game and the invitation of Existential Kink are to practice letting ourselves be madly, irrationally turned on and playfully excited by "strokes" in life that we would usually use to turn ourselves off.

So yes, Existential Kink *is* a bit crazy and strange, but it works.

4) Our degree of being "turned on" or "turned off" is a matter of how much we're willing to totally approve in our life

This axiom is thoroughly connected to the previous one, but it adds in the idea that turn-on is a matter of deep approval. Disapproval is alienating and distancing. It takes you out of the flow of interconnection and interrelationship and puts you into a grim isolation of resentment and disempowerment. But if you can let yourself get turned on about being resentful, well, you've just interrupted the pattern.

It's possible to experience exactly the same set of events in a way that's a turn-on, or in a way that's a turn-off and this includes the "internal events" of your emotions and thoughts.

How turned on and approving you are tends to have a lot to do with whether you're willing to playfully perceive your life as a wild, kinky game or whether you're hell-bent on taking it seriously and believing that it "should" follow a certain ego-pleasing pattern. The more you allow yourself to be "turned on," the less resistance you offer to the positive, creative current that's always attempting to move through you into manifestation.

It's possible to be sad, angry, disappointed—in a turned-on way. It's just a matter of giving yourself permission to fully feel the raw sensation that those emotions present, to meet the sensation with your innocence rather than your cynical judgment and "stories" about what these emotional sensations mean. In other words, it's magically useful to take an aesthetic, imaginative, artistic approach to your life and feelings rather than a dire, moralizing approach. Perhaps this is true because the great magician, God, is a Creator, and what is a Creator if not an artist, an author? Let's take the feeling of sadness as an example. An open, receptive approach to this emotion might be, "Ah, a deep heavy feeling of sadness, how exquisite. Hmm, let me feel into this, what is the texture, the sound? It's rather spongy, and when I pay close attention, I notice in my heart it sounds like a slow xylophone melody playing in a rainy alley." As opposed to, "Oh no, a deep heavy feeling of sadness. This must mean I'm a failure and my life sucks and I'm screwed. Everyone knows only losers feel sad."

The first attitude is a playful, aesthetic one. The second, a serious, moralizing one.

Try taking the aesthetic approach.

As Oscar Wilde once observed in a letter to a magazine in response to criticisms of *The Picture of Dorian Gray*, "If a work of art is rich and vital and complete, those who have artistic instincts will see its beauty, and those to whom ethics appeal more strongly than aesthetics will see its moral lesson. It will fill the cowardly with terror, and the unclean will see in it their own shame." Our trembling little human lives and emotions are exactly this—works of art that are "rich and vital and complete"—they're neither good nor bad, but deeply amazing to those of us willing to appreciate great and aching beauty.

5) Desire evolves through fulfillment, not denial and repression

We have all these unconscious desire-curiosities, and many of them are quite taboo and "wrong" according to the standard of our conscious mind. Some of these include the desire for scarcity and limitation, the desire to feel wronged, the desire to feel rejected, the desire to feel not good enough, the desire to feel offended.

Even though these unconscious desires are met in our lives by circumstances and events, we tend to miss a crucial step: celebration of fulfillment. We don't usually allow ourselves to consciously experience a turned-on sense of fulfillment and joy when these desires are met, because we habitually deny having them in the first place.

The longer we deny the fact that these dark, "fucked-up" desire-curiosities are a part of us, and that we enjoy their fulfillment, the more they continue to shape our lives. When we deliberately allow ourselves to gratefully feel, celebrate, and receive the fulfillment of our previously denied and disowned desires, we give those desires freedom. We give them space and light in which to evolve and change.

For example: once I've realized that I'm fulfilling my previously unconscious desire to feel "not good enough" through various dramas in my life, and I go ahead and (madly, irrationally) celebrate the fulfillment of that dark desire that's happening in my dramas . . .

. . . then that previously unconscious desire is free to morph into a desire to feel "good enough," and I'm free to move on.

6) Shame is the magic-killer

I can know right away that anything in my life, any attitude, any feeling, any situation I have shame about, that's an area of my life where I am accidentally suppressing my magic, and seeding the procreation of what we would call negative synchronicities—bad luck.

The more you give yourself permission to be shameless, the more the channel of communication between your conscious and unconscious mind opens, and the more effectively you can generate positive results. You are the only one who can grant this permission, at the level of your actual agency.

7) The truth is sensational

When we encounter truths that matter most in our lives, they tend to be highly sensational. I don't mean intellectual, abstract truths like 2+2=4; I mean profound emotional and relational truth.

For example, the first time we speak the words "I love you" to a romantic partner, our hearts beat fast and our cheeks flush. We feel warm and tender and excited and scared. Why? Because we're sharing a big truth.

If we stand within a sacred work of art like the Sistine Chapel or a Sun Dance arbor, we might tremble, sense an expansion in our chest, and feel tears brimming from our eyes. If someone confronts us with a character trait of ours that we don't want to look at, we might feel at first like we've been punched in the gut.

The fact that "the truth is sensational" matters a lot in Existential Kink practice, because as you explore the possibility that "having is evidence of wanting" you'll begin to notice that when your body is relaxed, it responds strongly.

For example, you might be doing the Basic Existential Kink Meditation outlined in Lesson 3, and say to yourself, "It's okay for me to feel my forbidden, wicked enjoyment of this custody battle with my ex," and as you say that, you notice that you feel a subtle electric jolt of sensation jump from your throat to your solar plexus. That jolt of sensation is important to pay attention to. It means that there's truth in your statement because the (profound, emotional, relational) truth is always sensational. *Literally.*

As you practice the Existential Kink meditation, you will likely experience a variety of sensations: subtle electric jolts moving from chakra-to-chakra (like the kind described above), sexual sparks, lightness, laughter, or tender grief. It's common to experience a wide, wide range of feeling and sensation in this work.

• • •

As you practice, I encourage you to accept that this is quite normal, and to pay great attention to what EK statements (explained in the section below on The Basic Existential Kink Meditation) are most intensely sensational for you.

Lesson 3
"EK"–The Basic Practice

This lesson includes:

The Basic Existential Kink Meditation

As we move forward in this book, I will explain a wide range of variations on this basic practice of Existential Kink that I'm about to outline below.

A wide range of variations on the practice of Existential Kink is possible because there are number of "approaches" or "angles" to any given kink, and because there's usually a sequence of "stages" of embrace on any given subject that we go through.

Note: I do not recommend doing this particular meditation if you are depressed, as it can degenerate into rumination. When you're depressed, other forms of *solve* work, like Deepest Fear Inventory and Inquiry, are generally much more useful. You can look to the Question & Answer section to see more of what I have to say on that topic.

Also note: there are many challenging situations in life that require immense deliberate grieving to move through, and I would not suggest attempting to do this work for a situation for which you have not first thoroughly grieved.

Please see the Question & Answer section in Part Three for more about the relation of grieving and hedonistic enjoyment.

Now, for the sake of present simplicity, here's "the gist" of Existential Kink practice:

1) Get yourself into a relaxed state.

Do whatever it is that helps you to relax. You could simply sit or lie down and breathe deeply for some moments, or you could precede your EK work by taking a nice hot salt bath or doing your favorite yoga stretches. Be flexible and experimental in how you go about getting yourself relaxed.

Relaxation is key. I recommend relaxing yourself as part of EK because the more relaxed your body is, the easier it is to feel subtle sensations flowing within it, and this practice is all about sensation.

Also, relaxation is nice.

2) Create a container for yourself by lighting a candle and some incense, and setting a timer for 15 minutes.

Creating a container means setting up some basic bounds of space and time to contain your experience so that you can more deeply sink into it.

When you have a container, you don't need to worry about getting "lost" in this far-out bizarro meditation, because you have set aside a special, finite time and place for it.

I suggest that you create a *spatial* container for this work by going into a comfortable room where you can close the door and not be disturbed. I also suggest that you create a *temporal* container for this work by setting a timer for fifteen minutes and lighting a candle and/or burning some incense. If incense smoke doesn't agree with you, you could spray some rose water or Agua de Florida.

The candle and incense elements here are arbitrary; you don't absolutely *need* them to do this work, but they are quite nice. If you consistently light the candle in the same space in your room every time you do EK, and if you consistently burn the same kind of incense (or spray the same scent), then these repeated sensory elements will become emotionally anchored to your practice and they will help you "drop in" to it more quickly.

Lighting a candle and burning some incense also signal to your deep unconscious that you are doing important transformational work, something special and outside your ordinary activity. Sending this kind of signal to yourself can help you feel more grounded and centered in the process.

After practicing EK in this concentrated, contained way for some weeks or months, you may find (as many of my course participants have) that you're eventually able to do it "on the spot" in situations that would have ordinarily felt unpleasant.

3) Identify a situation in your life that your conscious mind, your ego, does not like.

So, here I am, I see this sucky situation in my life—and I rather easily realize that my conscious mind *hates* it.

It's boring, it's limiting, it's ugly, it sucks: I want it to end and go away as fast as possible. I can't stand it, it's embarrassing, it's tiring, I want it to end.

Excellent.

Again, be sure that this is a situation that you have already thoroughly grieved. If, for example, you just found out that you're losing your job and your whole world is turning inside out, I would not suggest attempting to work on that situation immediately.

Instead, take time to thoroughly grieve this loss, to mourn your lost hopes and expectations. When you feel you've exhausted your tender grief around a matter, that's the time to practice EK on it, and not before.

Also, EK is best applied to "don't like" situations that are repeating, persistent patterns in your life. If you've been fired from three jobs for the same reason, then yes, that would be something to work on after processing your grief. If it's a bit of a random happening that you've been let go from your job, then perhaps just grieve it and apply your EK work to things that are more recurrent issues in your life.

4) Identify exactly what feelings and emotions you associate with this situation.

This is important because EK works best when we do it on the feelings, emotions, and sensations associated with a situation, and not on the fact of the situation itself. You see, the "don't like" situation itself is really just a by-product, a means-to-an-end, of getting ourselves to have the unpleasant feelings and sensations. Here's an example: one of my clients, Elsie, used to get tremendously anxious whenever she felt criticized or judged by someone in her social group. She practiced Existential Kink on the matter and discovered that the very same sensations that she had initially perceived as painful anxiety were actually kinky excitement.

This reminded me of psychotherapist Fritz Perls' famous observation: "Fear is just excitement without breath." In other words, fear is just excitement without embrace and approval for the sensations.

Through EK, Elsie discovered that she actually *loved* the intensity of attention and the feeling of theatrical momentousness that came with being criticized.

Indeed, it turned her on immensely. It literally created arousal in her body: flushed cheeks, a faster heartbeat—the same physiological response that comes from being alone with a lover.

When Elsie got very honest with herself and looked at her behavior, she noticed that she would unconsciously provoke people into confronting her with criticism because she got so much shadowy satisfaction out of it.

As Elsie allowed herself to consciously receive and savor the dramatic satisfaction of being criticized, to relish the excitement of it, she gradually lost the urge to sneakily provoke people.

Elsie realized that all along *she herself* had been inwardly criticizing and judging the people she hung out with as too boring and too uptight. So then she channeled the energy that she used to put into feeling anxious about being judged into finding a new set of friends that she enjoyed much more.

So you see, the "don't like" situation of "people in my social group criticizing me" was just a side-effect of Elsie's unconscious attraction to the emotional experience of anxiety/excitement.

When Elsie stopped resisting the sensations she felt when criticized and came to kinkily experience them as excitement, she lost the need to get her thrills sideways, and instead had the clarity to go seek out people whom she found to be just naturally more thrilling.

So to emphasize: focus on allowing yourself to take sado-masochistic pleasure in the *sensations and emotions* stirred up by your "don't like" situation. Don't put your energy into trying to get yourself to *like* the bare facts of what you "don't like."

Those bare facts are just side-effects anyway—you've put yourself in that "don't like" situation just to get the "awful" feelings that you hold so wonderfully dear. And that's quite brilliant of you.

5) Gently allow yourself to get in touch with the part of yourself that actually, passionately enjoys the feelings and emotions associated with your "don't like" situation.

This step of the Existential Kink meditation process is to take some time to gently, vulnerably allow yourself to get in touch with the previously unconscious, kinky part of you that enjoys this "don't like" situation. Consider that fear or aversion and desire always go hand-in-hand.

It's impossible to desire something without also fearing it a bit, and it's impossible to fear and dislike something without also desiring it.

Your enjoyment might be sadistic, or it might be masochistic. It's honestly hard to tell the two apart when it's something you're doing to yourself. Try experimenting with both angles.

Remember, "having is evidence of wanting"—if there's a situation or a feeling that's present in your life, no matter how awful it is, it's present with you not because it's "true" or "real" but because some part of the vast, strange, kinky Self that you are finds it fascinating, compelling, beautiful. And it's time to let that part of yourself and its taboo pleasures come to your conscious agreement and embrace.

Softly, temporarily put aside your ego and your usual judgments about who you are and what you want. To increase your self-honesty here, it can help to strongly imagine that the "don't like" situation will be utterly and completely removed from your life in just one month from now, as if "by the hand of God."

Since the "don't like" situation is going to be *inevitably*, totally removed anyway (you allow yourself to imagine), you can relax, open up, and allow yourself to feel just how very much a secret, taboo part of you enjoys it and cherishes it *right now*.

That part of you has been silent up to now because your conscious mind has been shaming the enjoyment of the "bad" things in life, like scarcity, rejection, and self-hatred. So you need to carefully coax it out.

Experiment with playfully saying the following EK statements to yourself:

"I'm willing to stop pretending I don't enjoy XYZ tremendously."

or

"I'm willing to allow myself to know about my secret, weird pleasure in XYZ."

or

"It's okay for me to feel my forbidden, wicked enjoyment of XYZ without having to judge it negatively or disown it."

You can also experiment with saying EK statements such as these:

"I'm totally allowed to have this weird enjoyment of XYZ. I don't need to shame it, I don't need to regret it, I don't need to deny it."

"I'm allowed to want exactly what I want, even if it's 'bad' or 'wrong' or 'destructive.'"

If you are able to get in touch with the forbidden throb of previously unconscious enjoyment, great! That's it! You're doing it!

Alternatively, you can take a coy, indirect, teasing approach to help disarm the defenses of the conscious mind. So sometimes in EK I like to say things to myself with sexy sarcasm (as if begging a devastatingly hot Dom not to whip me):

"Oh *no* no *no*, not feeling *wrong & bad,* anything but *that!* Please, please, no, I just can't stand feeling . . . mmmmm . . . *wrong & bad!*"

It's a bit silly, I know, but it works.

Often the enjoyment in Existential Kink can be felt as jolts of electricity or genital sensation. Just as often it can be felt as a movement of emotional energy. Sometimes it's felt as lightness and laughter, or just a soft sense of relief. That's "getting off" in Existential Kink.

"Getting off" in EK means that you successfully find your vein of previously unconscious enjoyment (and that you let yourself shamelessly celebrate it) in a deep way that gives a sense of release.

If, after some time of humorously, curiously searching and giving yourself permission, you don't feel like you can get in touch with the unconscious enjoyment, that's okay; you can still move on to the next step. I'll revisit excavating the unconscious enjoyments that are tough to "put a finger on" later.

It's important to note that some unconscious enjoyments require weeks of time and attention before they're willing to reveal themselves and be gotten off on. That's okay. Stay humble in the process, stay willing to honor the strange, dark pleasures. Eventually everything comes to light.

6) Get on the side of your shadow (your previously unconscious sense of desire/curiosity/enjoyment) and deliberately, consciously, humbly allow yourself to receive, feel big gratitude for, and get off on the situation your unconscious so brilliantly created.

This part of the Existential Kink process is crucial. Until you deliberately let your unconscious self fully receive and enjoy and delight in the situation and emotions she's creating (however "fucked up" it may be), that situation will just hang around and stay the same. The scarcity/romantic rejection/self-hatred will stay there, because your unconscious will keep just keep enjoying what she enjoys.

Why? because you haven't consciously given her the freedom to shamelessly receive and experience the fulfillment of her desire, to receive and delight in all the bloody, operatic, nasty, spectacular fulfillment of her perfectly reasonable enjoyment of scarcity/romantic rejection/self-hatred, etc.

It is through gratitude, deep receiving, and orgasmically enjoying the result you've already created (unconsciously) that you make space for your conscious and unconscious minds to sexually (magically) merge, fertilize each other, and eventually give birth to a new upward spiral of positive synchronicity in your life.

In this moment of the conscious mind humbly bowing to the desires of the unconscious, your conscious mind and your unconscious mind can finally meet. In this moment of meeting your unconscious becomes fertilized with the inspirations and ideals of your conscious mind. Your conscious mind befriends your previously unconscious pleasures and your unconscious mind reciprocates.

This is the alchemy, the moment of transmutation.

So decide that for just fifteen minutes you're going to humble yourself, set aside all your negative judgment, you're going to set aside your shaming and your egoic thoughts of:

"I don't like this," "I don't want this to be this way," "I want this to end," "this sucks" and instead you're going to savor and get off on your unconscious creation.

You can experiment with more EK statements like:

"This unconscious enjoyment matters just as much as any other enjoyment in my life."

"My enjoyment of this fucked-up stuff is just as worthwhile and important as my enjoyment of sunshine and roses."

"I honor this desire. I respect it. I'm allowed to enjoy this as exactly much as I do."

"I embrace and receive these sensations."

"I'm willing to feel the depth of my love for this."

"I open up to feeling wild, insane gratitude and excitement about these sensations and this situation."

This is the "kink" part of Existential Kink. In BDSM kink, people get off on things that they normally don't like. Pain, flogging, being bossed around. Well, in life in general, we have the same opportunity to interact playfully with pain. All we need to do is shift the context in our imagination from one of "awful thing happening to me against my will" to "kinky fun thing happening that I fully consent to." Get off on this thing, this situation, this feeling that your ego thinks that you hate. Feel the freedom of that, the liberation of it. Allow yourself to be touched by the magnetism and electric spark of the "awful" thing that's present.

The more you engage in this process of Existential Kink meditation, the more you drop identification with your ego and start to identify with *the whole* of who you are, with your soul and with your spirit. This is the *unio mentalis*, the alchemical marriage.

As your identification changes, you get a different perspective on life, and you start to see that *you always and without fail* create what you most deeply (unconsciously) enjoy. It's just that your whole divine Self is curious about and hungry for *all* incarnate experience, not just the "nice" ones.

Sickness and scarcity and death and grief and pain and loss and violence and weakness——all of these are fascinating, worthwhile experiences that the conscious ego-personality likes to judge as "wrong" or "bad" somehow.

Well, they're not wrong or bad; they're part of the panorama of life, and the unconscious divine Self that we all are wants to experience *everything*; it deeply wants to experience it *all.* Otherwise, why would the Self that we are have bothered to incarnate into duality?

This material world we live in is a world of polar opposites—love and hate, joy and grief, hot and cold, night and day, wet and dry, birth and death, health and sickness. If the Self that we are didn't want to experience all of this dizzying array of polar variety, it would have just stayed floating in cosmic undifferentiated bliss.

But as it happens, our Selves are more adventurous than that. The more you get on the whole Self's side and allow her to enjoy her experience of both pleasing and scary things, the more you can shift your identity from that of your isolated ego, to your Whole, Divine Self. And the more joy you can have in your life.

Future-Oriented EK

It's possible to do EK not only on currently existing conditions in your life, but also on things that you fear, and on things that are useful, but uncomfortable or unpleasant for you to do, like giving a high-stakes presentation at work or talking to a friend about a sensitive issue.

Here's how it works:

If you find yourself feeling anxious or fearful, practice the meditation on your imagination of what it would feel like if the thing you're anxious about *actually happened.* This veers out a little from the "having is evidence of wanting" idea in that you're working not on what's already present in your life, but on your worry about something that *could* happen. For example, I used to get anxious about failing and disappointing people somehow.

So for me, the practice was to imagine that *I had already failed and massively disappointed someone,* and then to work on letting myself get off on the sensation of humiliation that I imagined would accompany such stuff.

Usually when I do this, I notice just how closely entwined fear and desire truly are.

Any time I'm anxious about something, I'm actually tenderly caressing the possibility of it, pushing on it with my tongue like it's a loose tooth, savoring the little jolts of misery it gives.

Like "Ooooooh, what if I somehow forget something totally important and then I just FAIL and everyone, the whole internet, just *hates* me, for good reason, because I completely suck. . . ." You get the idea. I was basically obsessed with how hot and vulnerable it would be if I totally screwed something up. So when I really let myself feel that, it helped make it clear to me that my anxiety is something I *choose to do to myself* instead of some horrible automatic fate I can't control.

And then once I saw that, it was a lot easier to let it go.

You can also do this kind of future-oriented EK on discomfort associated with completing tasks that you usually avoid, but that you know are good for you, like deep cleaning your home or cooking and eating lots of vegetables.

This is incredibly important, because we humans tend to make our worlds and our horizons very small just to avoid discomfort. We put off doing tasks that are key to maintaining our well-being and fulfilling our goals. For example, for years I truly hated abdominal and core exercises. I hated everything about them. Flailing around on the floor, the burning sensation in my muscles, feeling weak and awkward. So I would avoid them. And, of course, lacking a strong core is not good, and I ended up with an achy back. All wellness folks I knew told me I needed a stronger core.

Ugh.

So, I practiced doing EK on the pain and awkwardness that I imagined I would feel in doing core exercises, taking perverse pleasure in it. I reminded myself that going right into my aversions is how magic happens. A part of me still hates core exercises (and what a joy it is to hate them!), but by perversely savoring my awkwardness and hatred, I've also gotten my core much stronger than it's ever been.

Note: While getting off in Existential Kink *does* result in a synchronous change of outward circumstances, it's very important that you let kinky enjoyment, pure and simple, be far, far more important to you than the "change" that you consciously want to bring about.

Why? Because if you're trying to get off on something just so you can get rid of it, well, then you're not really getting off on it, are you?

Instead, you're just faking an orgasm to try to appease your unconscious so it will stop bothering you and give you the good stuff. That's manipulation, coercion, and it simply doesn't work. Your unconscious knows you too well for that. You can't trick it. So let go of your attachment to outcome. Let go of doing Existential Kink so you can "get the good thing you really want."

Remember, it's very possible to "have everything" and still be miserable. That's why enjoyment, pure and simple, is always what truly matters.

And enjoyment, happiness, bliss—that's what you actually want "the good stuff" to give you, isn't it?

So just let yourself have the enjoyment, the happiness, the bliss right now in the midst of so much in your life and psyche being highly imperfect and fucked up.

After all, "highly imperfect and fucked up" is the signature of duality, and it's exactly what you came to this realm in order to experience; otherwise you'd just have stayed swimming in the cosmic soup and would have never bothered to come down into defined material form at all.

So go ahead and love it, you nasty freaky thing, you.

Let kinky pleasure be its own reward and don't worry about "trying to fix your life with integration." The mind tends to say that you'll be allowed to have bliss once you get everything sorted out—once you're fit, financially secure, romantically adored, etc. etc. This is just the mind's hot, fun way of torturing you!

The truth is you're allowed to experience bliss all the time, whether you're lying in a gutter, getting yelled at by your boss, getting ignored by your date, whatever. Your unwillingness to let yourself have big fat happy pleasure until you get "the good thing" is the very essence of sado-masochistic self-denial.

Starting to see how this works?

Another note: It's best to do Existential Kink work when you're already in a good mood. It can be very tempting to try to do Existential Kink when you feel bad. After all, that's the pain you're supposed to get off on, right?

Well, yes and no.

Doing this kind of work at a time when you already feel miserable can often just result in rumination or self-blame, and that is emphatically not what this practice is about. No one is "to blame" for anything—everything just is for some unfathomable reason . . . and we have the option of divinely enjoying it, divinely grieving it, or humanly resenting it.

When you're already in a bad mood, you're already so absorbed in your kinky game that you're identified with it, you've forgotten that you're playing the game or have the ability to play the game. In these states, it tends to feel like "I don't have a choice" or "it's being done to me." You've temporarily given up your sense of perspective.

Rather than trying to claw your way back to perspective by gritting your teeth and telling yourself you *like* your grim mood, it's wiser to first cheer yourself up by ordinary means—watch comedies, take a nice bath, talk to a good friend, listen to music you like, eat a nice meal, take a walk—and then, once you're again feeling more expansive, leverage that sense of perspective and possibility by applying it in Existential Kink.

When you're in this more expansive, good-feeling condition you'll still be able to contact the "don't like" situation, and you'll be able to see and celebrate your part in curiously creating it.

Gradually, you can link your expansive sense of choice to your awareness of the "don't like" situation in such a way that you become less and less prone to experiencing it as something that's "being done" to you, and more and more as a funny game you play, until one day it just dissolves.

Experiments

1. Practice Existential Kink

Each day for the next two weeks, identify a situation that you don't like in your life, and spend fifteen minutes applying the steps of the Basic Existential Kink practice.

I suggest that after every session, you briefly record in a Magical Diary (a journal) the topic that you worked, and how it felt in your body. Note whether or not you felt some degree of "get off" or pleasurable release on the topic. Write down any insights that come to you.

If you feel resistance, notice the story your resistance tells. What's the "good reason" why you won't let yourself totally feel the pleasure?

Work the meditation on the story of the resistance with some playful suspicion.

2. *Working with guilt*

Probably the biggest barrier to "getting off" in Existential Kink is feeling so much guilt about an unconscious enjoyment that we tighten up and thus refuse to feel the enjoyment and make it conscious.

With especially sticky unpleasant feelings, like guilt, it can be tough to feel the pure underlying, kinky *desire* for that feeling, but it can be simple to get in touch with *the motivation* for that feeling if only we're willing to investigate. And if you think about it, finding the motivation for something is quite similar to finding the desire for it.

You see, every unpleasant feeling we have has an unconscious motivation. Some part of us believes that by feeling the yucky feeling, we'll "get" something that will enhance our survival.

This part of us who believes in the survival value of yucky feelings was generally correct in childhood, and there it got a lot of validation for its theories (people came and took care of you when you cried!), but the theories of this part of us are generally incorrect in adulthood, where feeling bad just drains your energy instead of winning the help of caretakers.

So feeling bad/guilty/wrong as an adult doesn't actually improve your odds of physical survival, but it *does*, however, guarantee the survival of "you as you currently know yourself to be."

In other words, if you lost your ability to feel bad, you might hardly recognize yourself. You'd be stepping into an unknown horizon. You might risk offending people in your life who expect you to feel bad and who believe that certain situations *require* feeling bad. None of this would actually kill you, but it would kill your old idea of who you are. You'd experience a major ego death and transformation.

In these situations, I find that inquiry processes are of great help. So try this: ask yourself these questions slowly (inspired by the Sedona Method, which is a form of inquiry I often use as a warm-up to Existential Kink, along with The Work of Byron Katie and The Option Method), and contemplatively feel into the answers:

- Does this feeling of guilt come from a sense of wanting to control the situation?

- By feeling guilty, do I think I'll somehow change the situation, or at least get the approval of others?

- Am I willing to stop trying to use this feeling of guilt to get a sense of control?

- Am I willing to stop trying to use this feeling of guilt to manipulate others into approving of me?

- Would it be okay if the ability to use guilt to get approval or control just left me?

- What would it be like to live my life without ever using the feeling of guilt?

Phrasing the questions this way (talking about "using" the feeling of guilt to get something) may seem strange, but it's more honest and helps to make your underlying volition in the matter conscious.

3. The Game of an All-Powerful Being

Write in your journal in response to this prompt:

> Notice that the making of drama, of theater, of fiction, is one of the great pleasures of human life. From the pettiest gossip to the most refined tragedy, all dramas come from the same exquisite impulse to feel the fun of tension, conflict, uncertainty. Imagine that an all-powerful being has freely decided to be you, in your life, exactly as it currently is.
>
> Writing from the perspective of this all-powerful being, explain what dramas and games and fictions are being played out in your life.
>
> What motivates the game? What are the pay-offs?
>
> Who are "the evil-doers," in the drama, the adversaries in the game?

Here are some example answers to the prompt:

> *As an all-powerful being, I currently find it richly entertaining to play a game wherein it seems my ultimate value and strength are dependent on what other people think of me.*
>
> *. . . so I need to meet certain qualifications to "prove" that I'm valuable and "win" the game. Other people and the judgments that they have are my adversaries in this game.*
>
> *I'm trying to be so perfect that "they" can't possibly negatively judge me.*
>
> *When I play this game, I work myself into a state of feeling anxious and spread-thin. Whenever I fail to meet "the qualifications," I get to feel guilty and afraid.*
>
> *The more I do this, the more separate and alienated I feel.*
>
> *It's amazing.*

Or:

As an all-powerful being, I delight in pretending to be greatly offended by my partner so that I can put her in the role of "the evil perpetrator" and experience myself as a powerless, put-upon victim.

Then, from my position of pretending to be powerless, I get to feel righteously superior to "the bad one" who offends me.

Furthermore, I then get to guilt my partner, "the bad one," into doing what I want her to do so as "to not hurt me worse."

Then, I get to dislike myself for being so powerless and victimized, because that means I'm failing to meet "the qualifications" that prove that I'm valuable and strong.

Now I feel completely disconnected.

It's fascinating and delicious.

Or:

As an all-powerful being, I like to relax by pretending that I'm limited by my past actions and decisions.

I play a game in which my own invisible "past self" is the adversary, and I passionately hate her for all her wrong choices.

This way, even if there's no one else around to put in "the evil one" position, I can still put my own invisible past self there and still have my drama of being the powerless, wronged one.

It's such a huge relief to work myself into feeling weak and wronged and alone this way.

Etc. . . . you get the idea—see what you come up with!

Stories of
Transformative Experiences

Family Healing—*Angela*

There was something about EK that resonated deeply with me the first time I heard Carolyn explain it. The concept was not entirely foreign to me. I had been fascinated with the subjectivity of pleasure and pain my entire adult life. . . .

But this was a whole different level—enlightenment through the integration of unconscious taboos.

Like so many of us on a magical path, I come from a violently abusive upbringing.

Up until now, my main mode of interrupting the familial patterns was to stay out of contact. The thing is I was still angry and bitter and trapped in this weird pattern of poverty that I knew somehow had to do with my relationship to my family. In a wonderfully synchronistic turn of events, around the same time I started EK I also returned to my family of origin to help care for my elderly grandparents. Right there every day was my abusive grandfather, giving me a plethora of "don't like" feelings!

I begin by recalling all the times I had felt disrespected by my grandfather in the past and that expanded into all the times I had felt disrespected by anyone. I allowed all the sensations that came with those memories to arise: the anger, the embarrassment, the powerlessness, feeling weak and small.

Very gently I paid attention to the sensations in my body. Very gently, I said to myself, "having is evidence of wanting." And very shyly something new and different appeared——it was an enjoyment and a power in the background of those memories. A distinct feeling that a part of me brilliantly created and very secretly craved each of those experiences. It took me a little by surprise, and also felt so very true. Then, behind that, something else arose—frustration—the frustration of having what you want but not really being able to enjoy it. You know the frustration when it's been weeks since you and hubby have had any sexy time and there you finally are, in the throws of passion, your orgasm is imminent . . . and then the baby cries . . . that kind of pent-up frustration . . . I could feel this shy, deeply hidden part of myself feeling very frustrated. I apologized. I apologized for denying, for withholding, for shaming, for ignoring, for judging. For the first time, I allowed myself to feel a power that I had always sensed, but stayed away from. I was fascinated and also terrified—it was an enormous amount of power. And then it hit me like a ton of bricks: this "other" part of me has been running the show for a long time. This part of me has always gotten what she deeply desires. It's so difficult to explain a nondual experience when all we have is dual language. I was frightened by myself. I lay in bed terrified by my own power—my dark, manipulative, diabolical, destructive power. I've heard that the body's physiological response to fear and excitement is the same . . . I was terrifyingly turned on—by my own vast darkness.

The next day I sat in my grandparents' driveway, mentally preparing myself with this newfound freedom and power, when my grandfather knocked on my window. I stepped out of my car, worried that something had happened, and then something did happen . . . a miracle.

My abusive, violent grandfather who to my knowledge had never uttered the words "I'm sorry," apologized to me. I nearly fell over. And then the man who had never touched me other than to hurt me, reached over and brushed my hair off of my shoulder. I was flabbergasted.

That evening when I got home I suddenly had the urge to go through a box of family pictures. A box that I had carried around but avoided for years because of the "pain" I felt when I looked through it. I let myself feel and connect with each family member in the pictures, saying to myself, "I have a choice; I can choose pain OR I can choose pleasure" and then as I gazed at my family members I said, "You are a part of me; I accept you just as you are.

. Thank you." And just as shyly as before, that distinct power and twisted enjoyment emerged. I gave permission to the glee and before long I was laughing. I laughed long and hard.

The next morning, lying in bed, I thought, "I'm going to stop pretending that I don't enjoy being codependent. I give myself permission to enjoy being codependent." I just kept allowing, kept giving permission. The longer I stayed with it, the more pleasure I noticed in my body, so I began to self-pleasure and when I came I shouted, "I'm allowed to enjoy all of it! I can have all the pleasure I want! However I get it!" And then I wept with relief, huge relief. That "other" part of me felt seen and acknowledged and honored and the shame that was there dissolved.

After that I began to organically go into EK whenever I felt a strong "don't like" come up. Sometimes I would "get off," experiencing some kind of release of energy; laughing, crying, shivering and in general I was feeling lighter. A lot of days I still felt victimized by my family and I was still fervently trying to change them. Also, my financial situation began to shift, subtly, so subtly it took awhile for me notice. I had "out of nowhere" gotten two new clients and was able to save some money—both things I had been "trying" to do for months.

Then suddenly one day I was hit with panic; "I'm not doing it right, I haven't been doing it right! It's been too easy! I must have skipped something! It's working too fast! So I must not be doing it right!" ... and then I saw it ... my deep, overarching desire and creation of the experiences of smallness, deprivation, powerlessness, helplessness, embarrassment, loneliness, drama, pain, addiction, destruction, suffering. I was taken back to my times as an escort. Those sacred moments when a brave client would open up and share with me their darkest desires and most shameful requests. I remembered the reverence I felt for their courage and vulnerability. I remembered that All Accepting energy that I drew upon to dissolve their shame...and for the first time in my life I provided that healing for myself. I turned fully towards my dark, destructive, twisted, terrifying power, and bowed in reverence and gratitude.

My mantra after that was "You are allowed to crave whatever you want to crave."

I continue to practice this deep honoring and accepting. I sit and talk to this "other" part of myself, always approaching her with curiosity and reverence and appreciation. Relations with my family continue to heal and evolve, as does my financial situation. I'm not saying it's all turned to roses. Life is still life. What has changed is my belief in my power to influence life. I feel like I have been truly liberated from suffering.

Work Breakthrough—*Dahlia*

Work had been a precarious tightrope for me. I had always been ambitious and wanted to succeed, but I'd hit a certain level and stayed there, mired by my inner critic, insecurity, and self-consciousness.

So I decided to EK on my work life. Everything about it, all my frustrations and disappointment. At the last place I'd worked, my boss was a powerful, very rich, very charismatic man who'd built his company from scratch. I felt I had let him down and that was a painful thing to touch. I felt I owed him amends.

I meditated on that pain. I focused on my feelings of my incompetence and located them. I felt nauseous in the pit of my stomach. I let guilt and remorse flood my body. I thought about the ways that I hadn't dealt with my employer head on. How I hadn't followed up, how I thought I had to know all the answers and didn't ask for help. How I let my perception of his strength annihilate my own, how I allowed my passivity and inclination to be a passenger take over. So much shame. I wallowed in the feelings of incompetence, which I came to realize masked a desire to not take responsibility. If I didn't have responsibility I couldn't fail. What a glorious feedback loop!

Then I allowed love and approval and ecstasy to replace my acrid remorse. I felt full love for my timidity, passivity, and all the qualities I longed to cover up and keep in the closet. I realized the more I shamed them, the more they had come out sideways. I named them and brought them into the light.

In a moment of clarity, I recognized the metaphor in the waking dream that I hadn't seen before. And my former boss, maybe he was just another character I'd conjured up to embody the polar opposite of everything I thought I was.

Not long after, I received a call from an executive at a television production company. Was I available to produce a movie for them? "Let me check my busy calendar, "I said, already packing my bag. They were shooting a Christmas romance in a month and they needed a creative producer. We talked about my experience making Christmas movies and she promised to send me the script. A half hour later I got a call from the production executive with an offer and by the afternoon I was deluged by a flurry of emails from production.

I had to pinch myself. The happiest I'd ever been in my career had been on set rather than in an office. On set there's a singular focus that I found galvanized people in a more productive way and better matched my strengths of listening, inspiring, and sharing power. This was my dream job!

I received the script and sat down to read it. It was about a woman who returns to her hometown after her sister dies, where she is able to excavate the past and forgive herself for past hurts and free herself up to fall in love. Ha! It's all a bit meta.

I used to think success was based on how much you knew or how much experience you had, but I'm suspecting those are complete illusions of the material world. No one really knows anything. We're all just pilgrims on the road.

Car Triumph—*Louisa*

I used to ride around town in a hand-me-down junker, unknowingly killing my magic.

This car, a run-down 2003 Honda CR-V, had been passed down through my family for eleven years before it got to me. It was first the shiny new chariot in which my aunt would pick us up on weekends to go to the movies. Then, it was my mother's empowerment ride to escape an abusive boyfriend. By the time it became my first car, it had been through hell and back. No a/c, the driver's window wouldn't roll down, and the back trunk door was locked shut. Years of moving house had etched deep scars into the frame and boxes of donations my mother kept in the back started to mold. It also had a busted taillight. I hated this car. It smelled of mildew, cats, and poverty.

I was working at a high-paying and fulfilling job that made me dance out of bed in the morning before my alarm. Every day, I blended about $30 worth of high-end makeup onto my face, slipped on stilettos and my signature Versace sunglasses, and did my daily cat-walk of shame up to the dilapidated car.

Often, I would creep up to work with screeching brakes and park in between a Mercedes and a Jaguar, both belonging to people I'd coached to that level of affluence. I prayed no one saw me but I knew they all did. What the fuck? Was I a Witch or what? It was time for me to figure this shit out.

Although my husband insisted we couldn't afford a new car for another twelve months or so, I knew it was truly my own blockages that kept me driving the one I had. Even if we did have the money to go to the dealership that day, it was obvious that I'd repeat the same patterns and end up trashing the new car as well. It was time to destroy this demon.

That day, during my one-on-one with my boss, he asked me to commit to one tangible personal goal. I smiled wickedly and said, I will have a new car by my birthday (a few months away). I felt a calm surge of power, knowing that this was so.

That night, I played around with the idea of "Having is evidence of wanting," exploring how it was true with my relationship to my car. I wrote about how I felt driving the car in my journal: "I feel dirty, trapped, ineffective, poor, and shameful." A car did this to me? No. I did this to myself!

I had wanted this car so badly, once. I learned to drive in it and earned my freedom! But then I neglected it, soiled it, ignored it. Allowed it to deteriorate. Stubbornly refused to fix a thing. I created the condition it's in. I don't entirely know why. Maybe as a rejection of driving as a whole. Maybe as a retaliation of my childhood, and the attached feelings of entitlement. Maybe to keep me connected to familial poverty, that comforting container.

Realizing that I was staying very much in my head, I gently started to shift back into my body. I visualized myself inside the car, and breathed in that musty odor. I tasted it in my mouth. "Mmm . . . " In my mind I caressed every part of that car: the dusty carpets, the cat hair on the seats, the peeling steering wheel. I let the sensations of shame and repulsion build up inside me and wash over my body like an orgasm. Floating to the back of the car, I swam around in the moldy boxes, purring. The ants living in the air conditioning vents crawled all over my body. I let myself feel dirty and poor and irresponsible.

"Shame is the magic killer." I saw myself literally riding around in my stinking shame. The hairs on the back of my neck started to rise as I realized how much of an imposter I felt like, stepping out of this shitmobile dressed to the nines, to sell a glittery lifestyle to impressionable sales reps. I allowed myself to truly feel being seen and "found out."

The next morning, I woke up feeling light and practically bounced on my walk to the car. I took a few moments to sit inside, for real this time, and bring up all those feelings from the night before. I found it was harder to do because I simply felt at peace. I thanked the car for its many lessons and sang loudly on the way to work.

Soon after, I took the car to get it professionally cleaned. The goal was to make the most of what I had, and love her at her best. I emptied out the interior as much as possible and let the pros do the rest. It must have worked, because not even two days later, the a/c spontaneously kicked on during my morning drive. I nearly crashed! It had been out for almost two years! It worked beautifully for about a week before dying again, and I took that as a huge sign I was on the right path.

As I noticed my context starting to shift, I realized it was time to start envisioning the car I would ultimately want. In my journal I wrote, "my car is a 2017 black Tesla Model S. It's shiny and clean, with dark tinted windows and a fresh interior. The inside smells faintly of lavender and leather. When I drive it, I feel peaceful, powerful, sexy, and safe. I receive this car on or before February 23rd, this year."

Knowing that I wouldn't realistically be in the market for a Tesla within a few months, my conscious mind kept interjecting with more practical ideas like a Honda Civic or a Nissan Juke. It would be wise to be more practical, I resigned as I neared my deadline. Just as I'd decided that I was at peace with keeping this car for longer than I thought, my husband told me to shop around online for a BMW 3 series. "Pff, OK, a BMW," I scoffed. "Just look," he insisted.

Lo and behold, there she was, on the first page of the Car-Max website. Perfectly priced within our budget and within 100 miles, the process happened so quickly that I had the key in my hand within days. My heart was skipping as we drove her home for the first time. My husband turned and asked me, "So what's her name?" Without a second thought, I exclaimed, "Black Magic Woman!" We jammed out to Carlos Santana all the way home.

Black Magic Woman has been mine for exactly six months now, and although she's not a Tesla, I can proudly say: "My beloved black car is shiny and clean, with dark tinted windows and a fresh interior. The inside smells faintly of lavender and leather. When I drive her, I feel peaceful, powerful, sexy, and safe."

If that's not fucking magic, I don't know what is.

Part Two

Getting Kinky

"One does not become enlightened by *imagining* figures of light, but by making the darkness visible."

—CARL JUNG

Projection

In part one, we delved into the basics: the shadow and the unconscious. But before we get kinky with it, there's one more important concept that figures in the mix: Projection.

Imagine this: your mind is a holographic film projector.

The film that's playing is in full color and imprinted with all of your conditioning, all of your identity, all of your habitual patterns, every truth you would like to grasp onto.

The light that shines in the projector is the light of consciousness itself.

The big light of consciousness flows through the film that's colored with your conditioning, your beliefs, your habits, and identity—and through this filter the light of awareness projects all around you a hologram movie which contains precisely all those things inscribed on the film.

If you think about it, everything imprinted on that film is actually a kind of *shadow*. It's there to block or distort the light into a specific shape, so that there's something to be projected—so that we *see* the world.

Proof yet again of the power of the shadow: it's actually wonderful, for without the shadows printed on the film, there would only be a shining, pure light without form and without shape.

Shining pure light is nice and all, but it does not make for a riveting cinematic experience, that's for damn sure. One might say that pretty much every spiritual practice on earth is designed to one way or another stimulate our recognition that this holographic projection is happening.

Once we recognize that it's happening, it's actually fairly simple to realize that the consciousness that shines through each of us as individuals *is the same consciousness* that shines behind all projections.

This is an awesome place to start. It's illumination.

What can be a lot trickier to recognize and accept is that we're also the artist who put the imprints of conditioning on the film in the first place. Indeed, who we perceive ourselves to be and how we experience the world around us is entirely the result of that deliberate artistry.

The recognition and acceptance of our role as artist of the shadows on the film is a tad bit more exciting than spiritual illumination. Accepting our power as world-making artists and learning to consciously engage it is . . . drumroll, please . . . magic.

But what if we don't recognize the "out there" as being a projection of the "in here"—the product of our own creation?

"Negative" projection is one of the main mechanisms of the human psyche and it's a tricksy, tricksy thing, because it creates a certainty that whatever problem we're facing is "out there."

As I've already mentioned, our problems always seem to be "out there": our partner, our body, our boss, our lack of a partner, our own past decisions, etc., etc., . . . whatever it is, the problem seems irrefutably to be something that's somehow *external* to what we have agency over in the present moment. That's how we end up feeling powerless, why it seems that we're just at the mercy of the mean old "out there."

This illusion can maintain itself seamlessly over many lifetimes, until we're willing to get *very skeptical* about our certainty that we're being insulted or condemned by "outside forces." This is why New Age slogans like "You create your own reality!" and "Like attracts like!" aren't all that satisfying or helpful when you're frustrated or suffering with a particular situation.

What those slogans tend to not address is the ancient tension in the human soul between the deep unconscious part of us *that wants to be separate* (and thus threatened, alienated, lacking) and the part of us *that wants to experience union* (and thus bounty, harmony, beauty).

Eros & Psyche

The Greeks had a great story about the epic alchemical work of resolving this painful tension in the human soul: the story of Eros and Psyche.

In the story of Eros and Psyche, the human Psyche is separated from her divine lover Eros and has to undergo daunting trials, including traveling to the underworld, until she can be united again with Eros and produce their child, Voluptas, which means "Joyful Pleasure."

We're all Psyche, and we all need to make that scary journey to the underworld in order to have our reunion with Eros and to then be able to give birth to the field of consciousness that is Joyful Pleasure.

Finding and healing the unconscious, lack-obsessed part of you *with deep erotic love* (not weak-sauce "acceptance") is the essence of Existential Kink.

That deep erotic love lets you inhabit your genuine, profound agency, because once your psyche is filled with eros (i.e., united, brought together in love), *your negative projections end* and you instead produce a field of deeply beautiful positive projections and synchronicities around yourself.

This is what I mean when I talk about "becoming magic" rather than just "doing magic."

Doing magic is great, but "becoming magic" saves you lots of effort with spellwork because the more you "become it" the more it just happens spontaneously around you, without effort.

And that transformative magic is what we're going to focus on in Lesson 4—the big one—thirteen individual exercises through which Existential Kink can change your life.

Lesson 4
"EK" Exercises for
Transformative Magic

This lesson includes:

- How to Get Your Shit Together

- Deepest Fear Inventory

- How to Beat Yourself Up (the Fun Way)

- How to Dwell in the Luminous Dark

- How to Stop Being Broke

- How to Feel Blissfully Happy (Even if You Don't Want To)

- How to Feel Your Real Feelings (Not Your Fake Ones)

- How to Not Take Yourself So Seriously

- How to Feel Good in Your Body

- How Not to Suck at Love

- How to Stop Pretending You're Not Enlightened Already

- How to Stop Torturing Others by Truly Appreciating the Art of Torture

- How to Dread the Wonderful for Fun and Profit

How To Get Your Shit Together

Many of us intelligent, spiritually inclined folk have had a profound realization: there's no "reason" to do anything at all.

Or as Bill Murray famously put it, both in the summer-camp romp, *Meatballs,* and in his elegiac dramatization of Somerset Maugham's existential classic *The Razor's Edge* : "It just doesn't matter!"

We're all just fluid swirling emanations of an endless nondual reality, so in an ultimate sense it really doesn't matter whether or not you pay your bills, find true love, save the world, raise a family, or get enlightened. There's no rock-solid, nonidealogical, dogma-free, pure reason to get in shape, go to the dentist, have a baby, build a nonprofit foundation—or anything else.

We get stuck when we look for "reasons" to motivate us to action, because some part of us knows that there simply is no "reason." Many brilliant, wonderful people spend years mucking around in this swamp, propping themselves up with half-assed "reasons" for living, like not disappointing their family or friends. Such half-truths may keep you limping along, but they won't prompt you to truly get your shit together.

Here's a truth that can:

You don't need a *reason* to do anything. Your own kinky, hot, fucked-up desire to do it is enough.

Here's an example: It's bullshit to exercise everyday "because" you need to fit into fashionable clothes, avoid metabolic syndrome, or match some Hollywood ideal.

You don't. You can dress schlumpy, have every single lifestyle-associated health issue under the sun, match no physical ideal at all, and still be infinitely loved by the universe.

You can also give a big "fuck you" to the world of perky athleticism while doing so, which in itself is a tremendously appealing "reason" to not exercise.

Or, you can exercise out of your own kinky, weird, fucked-up desire to exercise.

Here's another example: It's bullshit to become an entrepreneur and make a ton of money "because" you need to pursue your dreams, express your creativity, or get wealthy so you can help your community.

You don't. You could stay working at your job, not do any of that "entrepreneur" or "wealth-creation" stuff at all, and the unfolding fractal holograph of unending space-time would still be totally cool.

Also, you can give a big "fuck you" to smug capitalism while doing so, and stay righteously broke, which in itself is a tremendously appealing reason *not* to start a company.

Or, you can become a baller entrepreneur out of your own fucked-up, weird, kinky desire to do so.

See what I'm getting at here?

There's a lot of power in not looking for "reasons" to do things, because equally compelling reasons can be found for *everything*.

When you just *own* your desire, without trying to prop it up with reference to anything, you gain a sense of responsibility for that desire which can clarify all your actions and slice through the Gordian knot of your conflicts.

So here's my advice for getting your shit together: Choose just one desire to focus on for the next three months. Not your whole life, just the next three months. And it doesn't matter which desire you focus on—any little inkling of inclination will do. It could be anything from "get a new boyfriend" to "write a novel" to "make $100,000" to "liberate all beings from suffering."

Accept that there's no "reason" to pursue this desire.

Write it down in your journal: "I have a kinky, weird, fucked-up desire to _____ and I'm going to do it, just 'cause I'm a nasty freak like that."

So you're deciding, out of sheer absurdity, to go after it with full, gleeful insane zeal. It is your own freaky lil' thing.

Want what you want just 'cause you want it.

If the pursuit of what you want is challenging or takes you far out of your comfort zone as big desires tend to do, great, savor all that exquisite discomfort because—again—your desire is just your own lil' sadomasochistic trip, and nothing else, really.

Do Existential Kink on both the pain of pursuing your desire and the pain of not already having it, (i.e., the pain of your current "don't like" situation of not yet having the new boyfriend, or the completed novel, or the cash, or the liberation of all sentient beings).

I really just dare you to cherish both kinds of pain, as they're equally wonderful.

At the end of three months, if you've stayed focused on pursuing your reason-less desire, you will have your shit vastly more together than it is right now. At such a juncture, either decide to keep pursuing the same reason-less desire, or choose a new one.

It just doesn't matter.

EXERCISE 2

Deepest Fear Inventory

The idea behind Deepest Fear Inventory comes from Marianne Williamson's famous, wise observation in her book *A Return to Love*, that "Our deepest fear is not that we are inadequate. Our deepest fear is that we are powerful beyond all measure."

Many of us would do anything to avoid the intense sensations of having giant power.

Deepest Fear Inventory is an excellent support practice for EK because it helps us to identify our specific resistances to receiving the thing we claim to want.

Once you've done Deepest Fear Inventory for a few weeks, it becomes very, very clear that the reason you don't have the thing you say you want is not because "the world is cruel" or "I'm just not good enough to have it," it's because there's a strong part of you that's afraid of the thing you say you want for a host of reasons, that doesn't yet actually want it.

Deepest Fear Inventory lets you see just how divided your will is. And that's great; you have to see the division clearly before you can heal it.

Something very interesting about Deepest Fear Inventory is how boring it gets.

You do it every day for some weeks on subjects surrounding the same topic, and you find yourself writing down the same fears again and again.

Eventually these fears get so boring that they're nonsensical, and you just let go of them because they're no longer interesting, at all. In this way, Deepest Fear Inventory is like scraping off layers of rotting old paint, bringing your deep dark secret fears out of your unconscious so you can consciously get bored of them and let them go.

The process can feel a little monotonous but once you've scraped that layer off, it's off, and that set of fears doesn't have power over you anymore.

Instructions for Deepest Fear Inventory

To do Deepest Fear Inventory:

Write at the top of a sheet of paper (and yes, it is important that you write on paper rather than on your computer because you're going to tear this paper up into little bits):

Dear God/Universe/Great Behemoth (however you like to address divinity),

I hate and resent having _____ (fill in the blank with what you claim to want)

or

I absolutely refuse to have _____ (again, fill in the blank with what you claim to want)
- because I have deep fear that I . . .
- because I have deep fear that I . . .
- because I have deep fear that I . . .

Rapidly write out at least twenty fears associated with your resentment and refusal of the thing you claim to want. Conclude with a prayer requesting the removal of these fears (you can find an example stated below).

After you've written out your Deepest Fear Inventory, read it aloud to another person (it's cool if you can do this with a friend or partner interested in doing this practice with you).

Upon listening to your inventory, the other person should just say, "Thank you for your honesty."

Then you say, "Thank you for listening," and you rip the damn thing up into little pieces and throw it away. No "holding on to it" to "refer to later."

Just rip up those fears and banish them. Tearing up and throwing away the paper on which you have written your DFI is a symbolic magical act that sends a message to your unconscious: "delete these."

Note: If you notice that your fears include worries about what other people might do, be sure to turn that around in your inventory so that you phrase it *as your unwillingness to feel* (in a centered, turned-on way) the sensation of other people doing that thing.

So "because I have deep fear that other people will hate me" becomes "because I have deep fear *that I am unwilling to feel* the sensation of other people hating me."

Feel free to write about other sensations that you're unwilling to feel in a centered, turned-on way—but definitely turn around your fears about what other people will do. Why? Because this practice is all about looking at your internal blocks, your unwillingness, your refusals—because that's where your locus of control lives.

Example Deepest Fear Inventory

Dear Universe, I absolutely refuse to earn $10,000 a month . . .

- because I have deep fear that I am unwilling to feel the sensation of receiving that much in a centered, turned-on way.

- because I have deep fear that it's wrong to receive that much money when other people don't have anything.

- because I have deep fear that I am unwilling to feel (in a centered, turned-on way) the sensations of other people's envy or resentment.

- because I have deep fear that I'll spend it all on dumb stuff.

- because I have deep fear that then I'll be free to buy a lot of land and build a permaculture food forest and then maybe I'll want to have a baby.

- because I have deep fear that if I have a baby, then I won't be allowed to be an immature self-centered baby myself anymore.

- because I have deep fear that I will maybe want to move out of the city.

- because I have deep fear that if I move out of the city I'll miss it.

- because I have deep fear that my family will treat me differently.

- because I have deep fear that if I'm that rich I won't have a right to pout about anything anymore.

- because I have deep fear I already don't have a right to pout about anything yet I still do.

- because I have deep fear that receiving that much valuing would threaten my story about myself (that I'm bad, dubious, wrong).

- because I have deep fear that I don't know who I am without my story.

- because I have deep fear that I might turn out to be someone very different than I previously thought.

- because I have deep fear that I might grow a lot.

- because I have deep fear that I am unwilling to feel the sensations of growth and change.

- because I have deep fear that I would feel humiliated by receiving that much love and valuing.

- because I have deep fear that I am unwilling to feel the sensations of humiliation.

- because I have deep fear that something new will emerge in me if I feel that humiliation.

- because I have deep fear that I do not know what that something new is.

- because I have deep fear of the unknown and am unwilling to feel the sensation of uncertainty.

Dear Universe, I ask that you remove these fears. I pray only for knowledge of your will for me and the power to carry it out. Thank you.

And then read the whole thing aloud to someone and rip it up into little pieces and throw it away.

Super-Positive Deepest Fear Inventory

The basic Deepest Fear Inventory process as I've just described it to you is often best for folks just starting out with the practice.

After you've been at it for a few weeks daily, I suggest trying this variation: instead of writing down actual fears, mentally turn each fear into its super-positive opposite and then write that super-positive thing after "because I have deep fear that . . ." So, instead of writing, "because I have deep fear that I'll spend it all on dumb stuff," write: "because I have deep fear that I will spend it with great wisdom, and massively benefit myself and others."

This super-positive, turned-around way of doing Deepest Fear Inventory is immensely effective because it calls out the fears of the part of our ego that's invested in feeling separate and powerless.

This dimension of the ego actually fears us feeling utterly wonderful and doing awesome things, because the more wonderful we feel and the more awesomeness we accomplish, the harder it is to feel alienated, separate, apart-from-the-whole.

EXERCISE 3

How to Beat Yourself Up (the Fun Way)

We all know the not-fun way to beat ourselves up.

By "beating ourselves up" of course I mean feeling guilty, ashamed, and generally bad and wrong for a host of things that we do and do not do. As we learned in the Working with Guilt section of Lesson 2, we always have an underlying motivation for making ourselves feel bad.

It might seem like "feeling guilty" or "feeling bad" just spontaneously happens to you, but it doesn't. It's an unconscious choice, a strategy designed long ago by your child mind *to get you something,* namely, the approval of the people around you, whom you depended upon for your survival and security.

Your parents learned it long ago from their parents, and they've passed it down to you in a rich chain of ancestral tradition. What might start out in childhood as feeling bad about not cleaning your room or earning good grades, blooms later in life into feeling bad about accidentally missing appointments, not replying promptly to texts, not eating enough vegetables, and offending people.

The thing about guilt is that most of us continue to use it long after its value expires. There's no automatic alarm bell that goes off when we become able to fend for ourselves that alerts us: "Now is the time to stop mirroring the emotional dysfunctions of your family; continuing to make yourself feel bad for your 'sins' will no longer garner the sympathy of your caretakers, it will only drain you of energy and eventually sap you of the will to live." And even if there was such an alarm, how could it possibly interrupt such an ingrained habit?

Here's a way: make your cruel, self-sadistic "operating instructions" radically explicit.

Uncover your *real* values and commitments, the ones you actually already live by, the ones that actually govern your moment-to-moment actions and emotions, and fully, consciously embrace them, at least temporarily.

To fully, consciously embrace your sadistic "operating instructions" is to stop shaming your villainous sadistic aggression and instead to celebrate it.

This is how you can free up the psychic energy that's currently bound up in your "operating instructions" and make room to choose new values to live by.

Here's example "operating instructions" to get you started:

- I will guilt myself for at least three hours if I offend or disappoint anyone for any reason.

- Feeling supported and safe is utterly forbidden, no matter what.

- I must always find flaws with the people stupid enough to love me.

- I am totally, 100% committed to doubting my own value and worth.

- If I fail to meet any of my responsibilities, I will hate myself intensely.

- I am utterly not allowed to feel total self-forgiveness. Feeling a little bit of self-forgiveness is okay, but feeling total self-forgiveness is not allowed, ever.

- The more I reject my own work and being, the more I can get approval from authority figures.

- I completely agree that my value is fully dependent upon other people's perception of me.

- I decide to relentlessly shame and repress my aggressive and sexual feelings towards others so that I can only experience them as free-floating anxiety or depression.

- I am 1000% committed to insulting myself whenever I fail at anything.

- My deepest value is to feel bad about myself and to help my loved ones feel bad about themselves by relentlessly pointing out the ways they let me down.

Whew! fun, huh? So, what are yours?

Grab your journal and write out "the rules" of your day-to-day feelings and behavior in no uncertain terms, as if you were programming an android to have the same hang-ups and neuroses as you.

Next, try treating your list like "reverse psychology affirmations." Read these affirmations in front of the mirror in the morning with great enthusiasm or with a Disney villain cackle every day for the next week and see what happens.

Remember, the point of this exercise is never to bring yourself down. The point is to notice what inner sadistic prohibitions are already operating in you at a previously unconscious level and to make those prohibitions explicit and conscious by spelling them out, giving them your full conscious agreement, and savoring their extreme Villain-esque sadistic ridiculousness. When you make them totally explicit and experiment with consciously agreeing with them, you easily see how over-the-top gonzo nuts they are, and your heart just lets them go.

Take the sadistic operating instructions, "I am absolutely never allowed to feel good about . . . XYZ . . . (my worth, my body, my creativity, etc.)" Ridiculous, right?

You are *totally* allowed to feel good and loving and fabulous all the time, about every part of you and your life. But if you don't *already* feel completely good about XYZ, then it's a guarantee that there is indeed some major part of you that unconsciously already agrees and believes in the sadistic prohibition to not feel good about it.

So the trick is to make space and time to honor that sadistic part of you, to affirm the dictates of the Inner Villain in their full glory, to stop resisting them for a moment and instead to go along with them. When you do this, it's as if you allow your unconscious shadow to finally complete a dance that it's been trying to finish for years.

Our whole lives, our conscious minds have been resisting these prohibitions imbedded in our unconscious by family, culture, karma, etc.

But we know that just insisting "No, I AM allowed to feel good about my worth! I am totally allowed to feel beautiful and powerful!" doesn't work for longer than a hot minute, or else everyone who ever tried affirmations would be a blissful saint by now.

Instead, we must temporarily drop your argument with the inner sadistic prohibition, and instead to play with giving it your full consent for a little bit of time. When fully consented to, when not resisted at all, the inner prohibitions lose their hold (because they're only kept in place by our resistance to them).

With your consent, your previously unconscious sadistic prohibitions can resolve, thus emancipating the previously stuck energy in your psyche, which you are now free to put towards your creative endeavors.

Indeed, after you've succeeded in liberating some energy with this practice of "reverse psychology affirmations"—it's a good idea to deliberately invest that energy in some new specific project.

How to Dwell in the Luminous Dark

The luminous dark is a paradox of course, and so are we humans.

You could say that the ego creates a sort of "spotlight" of grasping attachment focused on getting the "good stuff": success, wealth, progress, admiration, love, etc.

Everything the conscious mind puts in this spotlight—were we to get it—would, we believe, gloriously prove that we're finally and truly the ideal selves that we think we need to be in order to be okay.

The spotlight of conscious thought shines on an idealized version of ourselves and our lives, the vision of how things "should" be.

And you may notice that when you and your life and the people in it majorly or minorly fail to live up to the idealized standards of the spotlight, fail to give you enough winning or love or improvement or cash or adventure or respect . . .

. . . you might get flooded with all sorts of sensations, including anxiety, rage, humiliation.

Why? Because the spotlight is bright and hot, and it casts shadows.

In the shadows, there is also a kind of grasping attachment that mirrors what's in the spotlight. In the shadows, there is a hot attachment to failure and humiliation and anxiety and rage.

The ego/conscious mind may think that it's frightened of failure and humiliation (in matters of wealth, love, body, creativity, etc.), but fear and desire ARE IDENTICAL.

In fact, the conscious mind worries about all this "bad stuff" and thinks about how to avoid it, but that worry is secretly (shadowily) a kind of erotic caress, an obsessive dwelling with rapt fascination on the face of the very beloved failure and humiliation.

What I'm suggesting is: Just let failure and humiliation (and all the "bad stuff"—anxiety and scarcity and fat and wrinkles and pain and ultimately death itself) be the cherished beloveds that they already are to you.

Just let them be your open, known, sought-out, celebrated beloveds, instead of your secret, shamed ones.

Be infinitely willing to feel and experience all the bad stuff endlessly because a part of you already *is* infinitely willing anyway.

You don't have to "try" to love all the fucked-up stuff in your life: the simple fact is that you *already do love it,* immensely.

All you need is honesty. Just be honest with yourself about the subtle erotic joy you get from dwelling on/fearing all the "bad things."

Be honest about how exciting it is that you'll definitely die, and in dying, you will totally fail to keep your ego projects in motion.

You're a complete failure no matter what. A dead failure.

When you do this, the spotlight switches off.

You're in total darkness. There's no spotlight and no shadow— just a luminous dark as you enter the unknown of the present.

In this minute of the unknown present—you're you *as you are,* your life is *as it is,* rich with the beloved "bad stuff" and also a dose of "good stuff." And that is enough, with no improvements whatsoever.

The luminous dark comes when you find the courage to stop grasping after that idealized self-image, and instead for a minute just be the being that you honestly are, the one gleefully enraptured with desire-fear of the "bad stuff."

"Hot damn, I am infinitely willing to feel every painful thing in the world! I'm the crazy, infinitely willing one!" That's who you are, simply, in honesty, already.

Not when you try harder, or "do it right" or get Enlightened. Right now. You *already* get off on all your shadow stuff, you just haven't let yourself know it yet.

This infinite willingness to be a completely un-ideal person in a completely un-ideal life lets your spirit land fully in incarnation on Earth (and by the way, incarnation is by definition "non-ideal" because it is manifest, and specific in space and time).

Landing fully, right here, right now, in incarnation, opens up the horizon of what philosopher Jacques Derrida called "the absolute future," the future unconditioned by past patterns.

It is through the absolute future that magic comes in.

Turn off the spotlight. Turn on the luminous dark. Open to the absolute future.

How to Stop Being Broke

Ah, scarcity. Few things taste more poignant, pungent, and savory than the delectable flavor of scarcity, and the panicked sensation of impending doom that goes along with it.

I know it well.

Let me tell you a story. Years ago, on one bitingly cold December morning, I stood rubbing my hands together in a long, miserable line outside the Greater Pittsburgh Food Bank. I was dimly anticipating some government-issued cans of chicken soup, when a strange little thought entered my head: *I wonder, if some part of me really, actually likes this.*

About a year before, I had graduated from the University of Pittsburgh with a PhD in Critical and Cultural Studies. I had studied and taught literature, psychology, and continental philosophy, but was essentially an English major.

There's a hilarious old joke about English majors that was not funny to me at all in those days.

The joke goes like this:

Question: "What can you do with an English degree?"

Answer: "Anything you can do without one!"

I was 29 years old, I had just spent seven years of my twenties ("the prime of my life!" I would bewail) earning a PhD from a fancy university, and now I was flat broke as I scraped by doing odd freelance writing jobs because no one wanted to hire me for anything.

Which was understandable, as my PhD meant exactly nothing outside of academia and it took a whole lot of, shall we say, creativity to fudge my experience as a student instructor into sounding like anything remotely desirable to an employer.

Accordingly, I was living on the couch of some very kind friends, earning about $1500 per month, eating thanks to the generosity of the Food Bank and associates who knew how to dumpster dive, and most of the time I felt wildly, exuberantly, endlessly sorry for myself.

I had imagined that by age twenty-nine I would be something respectable and glamorous, like a hotshot young professor at Columbia. In the life my teenage self had believed I was absolutely destined to lead at 29, I would sleep in a big bed with fine linens (like a cloud) in my Upper West Side apartment, rise, imbibe a dainty espresso, pen some pithy words at my mahogany desk, teach some wily undergrads under autumn trees, romance some poets, and then fall asleep again in a silk nightgown in my luscious bed.

Instead at 29 I slept on a creaky corduroy couch in a small Southside row house, woke to a mean cat named Monkey scratching my face (my friends were very kind; their cat—not at all), waited urgently to share the one toilet with my three housemates who liked long showers, and then spent my days frantically seeking some scraps of work.

And of course it was my own fault I had gotten myself into this broke mess.

After all the effort of earning a bachelor's, a master's, and a PhD, I had decided I didn't want to be a professor after all. In fact, I never, ever wanted to set foot inside an institution of "higher learning" ever again. Why? Well, put simply: because in the course of my education, I had discovered that more than anything else, I believed in magic, poetry, and the soul. That doesn't sound so bad, does it?

Except it was, because these are three things that the modern academy hates and decries, and my belief in them rendered me persona non grata in academia, a ridiculous raving idiot that everyone else could neatly ignore because, as my research had ironically taught me, the contemporary university, along with our whole modern culture, is based in the values of materialist science.

Actual science I don't have a problem with.

Materialist science, I do, however, have a massive problem with.

Why? Because it's a kind of pervasive doctrine of belief that presumptuously asserts that only the material world exists, that only things that can be objectively weighed and measured are real, and things like spirit, soul, heart, and magic are all sentimental, meaningless, primitive hogwash. This is an attitude that treats the world and everything in it as objects to be examined and measured and exploited. The idea that stars or animals or plants might actually be things we might relate to with intimacy and gratitude is flatly rejected.

In short, materialist science isn't real science because it doesn't hold itself open to possibility. It's already smugly decided that the bounds of what it can know must be all there is to know.

Anyway, I had let this disdain of mine be known around ye olde English Department and the next thing I knew I was out on my ass with no apparent prospects of glamor or respectability on the horizon whatsoever.

I wonder if some part of me actually really likes this?

The curiosity itched at me as I stood in line at the Food Bank—was it possible—as the popular Law of Attraction teachers say—that our experience is created by our desire?

And if that's true—as my readings of Jung and Freud had suggested—could it be that I had a really fucked-up, kinky, unconscious desire that was creating my rather sad conditions in life?

I went home that day after gathering my cans of government-issued chicken soup, and I began a process of inquiry into that strange little thought which wondered whether or not some part of me secretly desired the very taboo humiliation and anxiety of my poverty.

Eventually, about a year later, with much patience, much self-honesty, and much setting aside of shame and judgmentalness,

I discovered that, indeed, a previously unconscious part of me truly, truly loved my poverty and all the indignities that came with it.

Here's how that discovery happened.

I was working as a coach at the time, living in an attic room at a community house, and still just squeaking by, charging $100 per hour for my coaching, with about five weekly clients a month.

I knew several other coaches who (according to me) were not nearly as good at coaching as I was, who were easily making $1000 per hour. This baffled and enraged me.

Where *the fuck* were they finding people who had that kind of money to spend on coaching? I'd grown up surrounded by people who worked for nonprofits and made at most $25 an hour, before taxes, so $1000 an hour struck me as a staggering, insane sum to be able to command. I could have just left it at that: some people are stupidly lucky and have great connections to wealthy people and I just don't. It's only those stupidly lucky people are able to make a staggering, insane amount of money for their work while I just can't. But since I accept the basic dictum of magic—"as within, so without"—I decided to get curious about what it was within me that was seeming to condition my earning power.

I figured that even given systemic wealth inequality, my internal, personal resonance must be playing at least some role in creating the scarcity and impossibility I felt.

I decided to do The Work of Byron Katie inquiry process on this idea. The Work is a practice where you take a stressful thought and you question it, thereby releasing the grip it has over you, which eventually sets you free. I highly recommend it in conjunction with Existential Kink work.

I took the Judgment thought, *I need potential clients to be happy to pay me $1000.00 an hour* and according to The Work's classic protocol, I asked myself, *Is it true?* I couldn't find any resonant "yes" sensation in my body, so I answered "no."

Then: *How do I react when I believe that thought?*

I noticed I felt tight, panicked, lacking, anxious. Mmmmmhmm.

Then: *Who would I be without that thought?*

I got quiet and found that without the thought, I would feel open, light, more honest and present. Per Byron Katie's instructions, I turned the thought around, and looked for the way that my initial judgment was equally true.

I first "turned-it-around" to self, as in:

"I need *me* to be happy to pay myself $1000 an hour for coaching."

I was immediately struck with the truth of that statement. It stood to reason that if I wanted to be a $1000-an-hour coach, then I should be willing to invest $1000 an hour to be coached by someone else. I would later act on that insight, and it formed an important stepping-stone in my process of becoming a $1000-an-hour coach.

Next, I tried turning the judgment around to its opposite, which sounded like:

"I deeply need my potential clients to absolutely never, ever want to pay me $1000 an hour for coaching."

And then, something quite strange happened. I felt an electric zing and a big throb in my clitoris. It occurred to me, from all my previous life experience, that the truth is highly sensational. So I decided to explore this notion. After all, maybe I was feeling the zing of deep truth? I tried more statements along the same lines to see how they resonated:

"I am totally delighted to have people utterly refuse to highly value me."

"I love being rejected when I propose coaching offers."

"I really need clients to never want to pay me at all."

For each of these statements, my body strangely responded with throbs of pleasure.

The more I thought about other people absolutely refusing to highly value me and my work, the more aroused I got. Gradually it dawned on me: *Well of course I don't make $1000 an hour; I am so turned on by being devalued and rejected!*

Turn-on enthusiasm is always magnetic, and now I was sitting with the stark realization that I had unconsciously been magnetizing scarcity and rejection to myself all along.

It occurred to me that I had been unconsciously enjoying and magnetizing devaluation for years, but I had never before let myself know it because it's a shameful, freaky, weird thing to be turned on by devaluation and scarcity in real life.

I spent the next few weeks consenting to feel the kinky joy in my anxiousness about how I would pay the rent that month, the forbidden thrill of being financially scarce. As I noticed how much the anxiety and humiliation of scarcity turned me on, I also got very curious.

Was I actively avoiding the sensation of being highly desired, highly valued by my clients? Highly valued not just in a sentimental way but highly valued with cold, hard cash? As it turns out, yes, I was.

I realized that allowing a client to pay me $1000 an hour would feel intense, it would make my cheeks flush and my heart beat faster, and that I was afraid of that level of intensity, with that level of being trusted and—actually, economically—not just sentimental valued. I noticed that I had a kind of unconscious commitment to homeostasis—I only wanted to feel a certain amount of the already-familiar kinds of sensations (mostly miserable, turned-off ones) that I was used to feeling.

I actively avoided being confronted with unfamiliar quantities of unfamiliar sensations . . . like the sensation of having someone want to pay me $1000 an hour for coaching.

This unconscious commitment to homeostasis was my "havingness" level.

A havingness level is a kind of internal imprint based on past family and cultural conditioning that determines the amount and kinds of sensation that you're willing to feel before some part of you unconsciously decides it's "too much" or "too good to be true" and then goes into fight, flight, or freeze—usually for some highly fictional (but seemingly factual) reason. I mention this "highly fictional reason" piece, because usually when a person has a havingness-level freak-out, they don't realize that they're experiencing a havingness level freak-out, that too much hot sensation and too much good stuff is coming their way . . . instead, they usually think they're freaking out because "I suck," or "the world sucks," or "my partner sucks," "my client sucks," etc., etc.

In other words, the conscious mind "makes up" a fictional reason to freak out, one that convincingly hides the actual underlying reason that the freak-out is happening (the unconscious need to avoid too much good stuff), thus keeping the imprint intact, thus maintaining familiar homeostasis.

People have various sorts of havingness level or "upper limit" imprints based on their karma and their childhood experiences. Some folks, for example, are willing to feel highly valued with money but are totally unwilling to be highly valued with love, or vice versa. Other folks are massively uncomfortable with all kinds of "being valued" sensations.

Your havingness level is deeply connected to who you know yourself to be. I say "know" because when it comes to matters of identity, we don't deliberately "believe" ourselves to be something or other; we just feel like we "know" it.

I, for one, always smile a little when well-intentioned people tell me to "question my beliefs" as a means of opening my mind. I find it's much more liberating to question my "fundamental truths" because my most potent beliefs are the ones that I don't even consciously experience as beliefs, but just as "the way things are" and "who I am."

The point is: who you know yourself to be, right now, is a kind of fictional-yet-utterly-real-seeming blueprint that defines how much good stuff you'll let yourself have.

We humans tend to fiercely defend our identities as being "somehow separate and lacking" and feel deeply suspicious of any set of circumstances that would dare hint that we're actually whole and wondrous.

By imagining myself being paid "staggering sums" for my work, I practiced being willing to experience the sensations of being highly valued. And then I discovered something even more odd: as I consciously, deliberately got off on my scarcity kink and practiced growing my havingness level, I felt fulfilled and I simply lost my kinky hunger for scarcity, poverty, and humiliation. It just left.

I lost my ability to take my empty bank account personally. My poverty no longer felt remotely relevant to me anymore, either as a kink or as a sorrow. Instead, I would think about being paid a staggering sum for my coaching, and it no longer felt impossible or intimidating; rather it felt hot.

I started getting turned on by lots of money, rather than turned off by it. With this new kind of turn-on, I became willing to take mundane actions towards growing my business that in the past I had totally avoided, like building an email list.

Suddenly, business-growth efforts that had sounded too scary or too intimidating to me in the past looked simple and obvious. I found I had huge creative energy to take these steps. I discovered that all along there were things I could do, that were not that difficult, to rapidly grow my business. I simply wasn't able to even see them until I changed my havingness level. It felt like having a veil lifted from my eyes.

I was no longer able to regard my tiny bank account as a horrible sign of my personal failure mixed with how much the world hated me. Instead, it was quite obvious to me that my low funds were a deliberate, entertaining, adorable choice of my own inmost soul—the inner divine wholeness that Jung called the Self with a capital "S."

A few months into this, I started bringing in $10,000 a month rather than $2000. As within, so without. My whole world and horizon of possibility changed.

I still didn't have fabulous connections, but as I expanded my havingness level, I became willing to feel intense sensations and to put myself on the line in conversations with potential clients in ways that I previously had not been willing to do.

And I became attractive to a different kind of client—successful entrepreneurs who themselves had a higher havingness level around money began to gravitate to me. My creativity flowed much more potently after I accepted and integrated my shadowy desire for scarcity and lack. So I took the business-building steps that I had previously felt unworthy of taking, and then my outward condition changed, drastically.

Wow.

It's hard to overstate my initial (and ongoing) excitement at realizing that the fundamental dictum of magic ("As above, so below; As within, so without"—from the Emerald Tablet of Hermes Trismegistus) was true, and that inner states can indeed provoke miraculous changes in outer conditions.

This was extra-exciting to me because even though I had always revered magic, by listening to the mainstream Law of Attraction crowd and their insistence that it's possible to get what you desire just through visualizing and affirming it, I had begun to fear that magic was bullshit.

Why? Because the Law of Attraction ideas always seemed a little—well, how to say this diplomatically?—*extremely stupid* to me, but I could never put my finger on exactly why.

But now I could put my finger on precisely why: the usual Law of Attraction crowd strikes me as so dumb because they're only half-right, I realized.

We *do* always get what we deeply desire, but most of us aren't that aware that much of what we deeply desire is some highly unpleasant, painful, secret, repressed, fucked-up shit.

As it happens, the way to have profound success in altering your inner state and thereby altering your outer experience isn't through endless "positive thinking"—it's by being willing to look at the darkest, most twisted stuff in your experience and in your own heart and to feel great gratitude for it.

It takes a huge amount of courage, self-honesty, and suspension of negative self-judgment ("Oh, I secretly want a terrible thing! This means I'm a terrible person! Terrible, terrible, terrible!")—to begin to be able to see the vast depth of one's own kinky desire for highly unpleasant, painful, freaky stuff.

Let's say you've accepted the first axiom of Existential Kink as an excavation tool, and you've discovered that what you're "having" in your life right now is a bank account and income that hav you feeling broke.

Maybe you're stuck in a job you hate, or you can't find work that suits you. Maybe you earn a lot, but you seem to spend it as fast as sand falls through a sieve.

And let's say, like most of us, you're just beginning to understand that some unconscious part of you desires this situation, but you're angry about it.

Maybe you feel it's wrong or crazy that any part of your being would be so attached to feeling limited, helpless, bound?

Understandable. But. What if the previously disowned dimension of your being, which has a feverish abject lust for the umami tang of scarcity, is a beautiful thing? It's also a lot more fun than your lamenting ego.

This part of you just happens to be fascinated with the experience of constriction, in love with it, actually. And that desire is just as precious, sexy, and adorable as any of your consciously condoned desires.

So I invite you to take a deep breath and drop your judgment of the constriction this part of you has created. For just a few moments, I invite you to fully identify with this kinky part of you. For just about three minutes, let go of thinking that you're the one who disapproves of this anxious pauper scene.

Imagine that you're a kind of cosmic masochistic slut (and I mean that in the nicest possible way—*yay* sluts!) who just beamed down into your life and body.

She feels the heart-pounding panic of impending doom too, and *she loves it.*

She feels the pressure of having to find a way to make ends meet again this month, and *it turns her on.*

She feels the stretch and strain of having to prove herself worthy of support in this hard, cold world, and she *trembles and moans and asks for more.*

Plus, let's not forget—she feels the righteous resentment of the evil rich corporatists and politicians who made this world so unbalanced—and well, there are few things more luscious in this sublunar realm than a big stinging heap of righteousness.

Of course the thing is, that you *are* this cosmic pain slut— she's not strictly imaginary, you've just repressed and disowned her up to now.

How do I know that you're a cosmic pain slut? Because this material world of ours is the world of apparent limits, constriction, gravity, finitude.

You wouldn't have incarnated here if you weren't attracted to the rollercoaster ride.

Now imagine that the kinky, debasing, desperate pauper scene you've been getting off on just ends.

It goes "poof."

There are no financial chains holding you in bondage any more, no lousy boss, no need to prove yourself worthy of being paid.

In fact, you're rich. Wildly rich.

If you bought a platinum-coated jet every day of your life, *plus* fed and housed and healed all the billions of needy people on earth, and you'd *still* never run out of cash.

You're just that insanely, endlessly rich.

Notice what sensations arise as you imagine this.

Is there some numbness? Maybe guilt? Maybe overwhelm?

After all, now that you're no longer materially constricted, there's endless possibility.

You could live anywhere, do anything, create anything.

Plus, there's going to be people in your life who resent and envy your newfound wealth.

Is there a heaviness to all this possibility and change? Like, a lot of responsibility?

You could decide to walk away from it all, give your vast fortune away to a charity and go live in a hut in the forest, but even *that* is a big sensational decision that you'd be responsible for, isn't it?

Both scarcity and bounty are highly sensational.

The flavors of sensation that they carry are just a bit different.

You can choose to have all the sensations that go along with wealth, but first you need to get crystal clear on your fondness for all the sensations that go along with scarcity.

Why? Because if you keep truly believing that you "hate being broke" or "want to get rid of this anxiety about paying the bills"—you're likely to hold onto being broke and anxious about paying the bills, for the simple fact that the game is still totally absorbing you, because you won't let yourself realize *it's a game*.

Once you accept how thoroughly you cherish being broke and having this anxiety about paying the bills, the entrancing spell of the game is broken, and you'll find yourself drawn into a new game, with new stakes that are more mesmerizing than the last ones.

Like being a tycoon with the fate of the world in your hands.

So I invite you to spend some days or weeks really getting off on and relishing in the scarcity that you've already unconsciously created.

After you've done that for a while, to the point that you really *get* on a tangible, electrical level that you are indeed a glorious cosmic pain slut and that your scary pauper scene is fucking awesome, not to mention aesthetically *en pointe* . . .

. . . then I suggest that you brainstorm about some actions you can take to increase your income and improve your financial situation.

I promise you your creativity in this matter will be much improved after you've given yourself some time to lap up the forbidden fruits of your freaky financial torture scene.

Now, make a rejection game out of your actions.

The game is to do thirty iterations of your chosen action, and get as many rejections along the way as you can.

Let's say you're job hunting. Your game is to go apply for 30 jobs that would be a big improvement on your last one, and to get rejected as many times as possible.

Or, maybe you're a consultant. Your game is to have 30 conversations with prospective clients at double your old rates, and to rack up as many "NO"s as you can.

Or, perhaps you're an entrepreneur with a new app. Your game is to have thirty meetings with potential investors, and see how many times you can get shot down.

You get the idea. One action. Thirty iterations. As many rejections as possible. Go.

But.

Won't it hurt to get all those rejections?

Yes, absolutely it will; it will hurt *so bad*, you cosmic pain slut, you.

So I expect you to set aside at least fifteen minutes each day to really revel in all those sharp, piercing "no"s.

By the end of this game, you are likely to get at least a handful of "yes"es.

That's okay, you tried.

With some of these wins that you accidentally get, your financial situation will improve, maybe vastly.

That's all right. You now know what you need to know to enjoy the sadomasochism of being rich, too.

How to Feel Blissfully Happy (Even if You Don't Want To)

Once, in the midst of a harrowing adventure, a dear friend said to me: "Carolyn, tell me something funny!" I looked at her, with her eyes squeezed shut, and said, "What, the fact that we're all gonna die isn't funny enough for you?"

Her eyes opened with shock and then she doubled over with laughter.

Mortality is tragic, but it's also hilarious because it's so common and inescapable. We habitually think that we're our personalities, our bodies, our histories, our thoughts, our feelings, but all of that is just content, and it will all dissolve when we die. Ultimately, what we all are is the context in which our lives happen.

Even if people remember our life's story and accomplishments for thousands of years after our death, eventually, the last person who remembers us will die and then it will be as if we never existed at all.

Vanity is called vanity because it's *in vain.*

The essence of growth is to put more attention on context rather than on content. The content of who you are is totally ephemeral, utterly changeable. Your memory, even, is constantly changing and dying.

Go ahead—remember your first kiss. Then remember it again tomorrow. When you remember it again tomorrow, the experience of the memory will be different, even if just ever-so-slightly. Your memory of your first kiss is much, much different than your memory of it the day right after it happened.

The content always dissolves.

But the ultimate *context* of who you are remains, because the context of who you are is presence, awareness, consciousness, pure and simple. That consciousness doesn't die, just as the sun doesn't die when it sets. It's just that a new holographic movie, a new set of content appears within the eternal context. The fresh content is the afterlife, or your next life, whatever. Change of scene and character. Same stage.

Many would say that the content of your afterlife and your next life (heck, even your next five minutes in this life) has a lot to do with how aware you are that you are *in fact* the context and not the content.

It's very easy to get absorbed in content—almost everyone spends their existence completely hypnotized by their thoughts, feelings, stories, worries, doubts, and with trying to get the content to be "better."

The paradoxical truth, though, is that the content of our lives (and perhaps afterlives and next lives) becomes exponentially better not so much by worrying about trying to change the content that's happening but by coming more and more to know ourselves as the context—the awareness, the presence—in which all the content appears.

It's as if we just stopped trying to rearrange the furniture in our old shack and instead just move into a mansion. Easier said than done, right?

Yet in the basic Existential Kink process we've been working with so far, this is exactly what we do: we set aside our habitual one-sided concern with our ego's demand for only the "good" content, and we instead practice opening up to experiencing the whole content of our lives (the situations, the emotions, the thoughts, the stories—including the yucky stuff) from the fuller context of our total Self, which rejoices in everything, even the very taboo content that we usually despise.

In doing this we invoke Eros. The Chaldean magicians, whom some ancient Greek philosophers studied with, considered Eros, the force of love itself, to be a teletarche—a "master of initiation" greater even than the Olympian gods. The other Chaldean teletarches were Pistis, or Trust, and Aletheia, Truth-as-Unconcealment.

Among the teletarches, Eros is perhaps the easiest to invoke, because, well, he loves to be invoked, he loves to draw near, to link, and connect.

In Plato's *Symposium*, the philosopher Socrates quotes his teacher, Diotima, a courtesan, on the nature of Eros.

According to Diotima, Eros is the cherishing of divine beauty, "the beauty that is not beautiful and is not ugly." In other words, Diotima sees Eros as the love of the context in which all life and beauty unfolds, the formless context that is beautiful because it holds all possibilities.

When you succeed in getting off on a given topic in Existential Kink, you are succeeding in releasing your fixation on ordinary beauty (or the lack of it), releasing your fixation on the content of your experience, and instead opening up to the larger beauty "that is not beautiful and is not ugly"—the context, the fundamental love that is You.

What's more, you're opening to that larger beauty in a deep, embodied, electric fashion rather than on a merely intellectual level.

After becoming proficient in that fundamental "move," of Existential Kink—of getting off on "the ugliness" in such a profound way that it no longer strikes you as ugly, but as an adorable, funny part of the whole—the next step is to practice allowing yourself to feel, receive, and truly get off on how wonderful your life already is.

That's right. And I'm not talking about just some dusty old "gratitude" or "appreciation." I'm talking about soul-ripping, heart-pounding, genital-throbbing, gut-busting reception.

It might sound like it would be totally easy to get off on the wonderful stuff, but this next level of Existential Kink is a *practice* because most of us are actually very committed to dodging the most intense pleasurable sensations of life—intimacy, creative inspiration, being valued with time and money, being desired.

In order to dodge feeling these intense, wonderful sensations, we turn ourselves off, mainly by using worry, doubt, criticism, complaint, resentment, and upsets.

Now you may say, "Oh no, not me, I welcome all wonderful sensations! I wish I had more of them! I wish I felt more valued, more loved, more inspired . . ."

Right.

But do you *really*?

Isn't it a bit suspicious that you've been wishing for all this good stuff for your whole life and yet no matter how much you may have, the big, perpetual, longed-for fulfillment still feels just out of reach?

You tell yourself you might get "it" if you just worked hard enough, improved yourself enough, figured out enough—if you got the right relationship, the right career, or the right level of fitness.

But the real reason the big fulfillment still feels out of reach is not because you haven't gotten it yet. It feels out of reach because you already have it, but you're actively (unconsciously) avoiding it. Life, the universe, is already stroking you right on your most sensitive, hottest, most fulfilling spot with the situations and feelings present in your life right now.

But you won't let yourself feel or receive or even consciously know that the Big Fulfillment is right here, right now—because to do so would make all of that worry, doubt, complaint, and resentment utterly ridiculous.

And we can't have that, can we?

To experience total fulfillment right now would be humiliating. To realize that you are the person who (at least for this moment) really likes being stroked by life in exactly this way, *exactly* on this tender embarrassing spot—that's mortifying.

Allowing that realization would be an abrupt, rude curtainfall, and lights out in the middle of our grand opera of lack, longing, and doubt. The show would be cancelled right in the middle of the act. How shameful!

But if we get willing to have this abrupt, rude curtainfall happen without being ashamed of it, we can increase our capacity to have all "the good stuff" enormously, because our access to "the good stuff" kind of content comes much more readily when we're receiving the Big Fulfillment that's already here, when we're willing to get off on the sensitive, vulnerable spot that life is stroking on us right now.

Most of us have teeny tiny havingness levels.

Your havingness level is the amount of sensation and energy that you'll let yourself have before you unconsciously, automatically turn yourself off . . .

- . . . by getting worried, doubtful, judgmental, resentful, critical, complaining, upset . . .

- . . . by having an accident, an argument, a misunderstanding, a gaff, a horrible mood, a depression . . .

- . . . by any means necessary to give yourself an excuse to stay in the small, tight, homeostasis your familiar identity with the familiar content of your being—your ego, your personality, your body.

Try this:

A Simple Havingness Check-In

Close your eyes for a moment and feel into your current state.

Are you holding any resentments? Judgments of yourself or other people? Worries? Criticisms about the state of the world? Complaints about your body, your work, your life?

Is it possible that these judgments, complaints, criticisms, resentments are mechanisms whose sole purpose is to help you avoid feeling tremendously good, loved, valued, inspired?

"No, no, no—sure I have resentments and judgments and criticisms. I have them because terrible things have happened to me, terrible things are happening everywhere in the world right now, and more terrible things could happen at any moment."

Precisely so—we've all suffered great wounds, people are being wounded right now in all sorts of gruesome ways, and we could all be wounded by surprise at any moment.

And.

Those wounds are all part of the content, part of the opera. You are not the wounds, not the emotional reactions, not the content—and no one is. We are all the context, the opera house.

Of course that's a big realization to take in. It's the life-long project of the Great Work to understand and embody that realization fully.

But you can start right here, right now, to get very curious about the contextual processes behind your "stuff" and much less concerned about the surface content of it.

One way to do that is by closing your eyes, checking in with your state of being, and asking yourself, as we just did:

"Is it possible that these judgments, complaints, criticisms, resentments are meaningless mechanisms whose sole purpose is to help me avoid feeling tremendously good, loved, valued, inspired?"

When you're wrapped up in feeling miserable about something, it often seems that the content of what you're miserable about is very real and important.

What if it's just not?

What if it has no intrinsic meaning whatsoever?

What if whatever "problem" you're hung up about is just a vehicle for numbing yourself to the massive turned-on joy and fulfillment you could otherwise be feeling?

In Hindu mysticism, the subjective perception of ultimate reality is called sat-chit-ananda, meaning "existence, consciousness, bliss." (Side note: I'd venture a guess that these three qualities correspond to the teletarches, the "masters of initiation"— Pistis, to existence; Aletheia, to consciousness; Eros, to bliss.)

If, as I do, you want to take seriously the experience of thousands of yogis throughout the millennia who emphasize that the fundamental nature of existence feels like bliss (i.e., Eros, pleasure, enjoyment), then it's worth getting really suspicious about your relationship with reality whenever you're not blissful.

In other words, if the content of your experience feels awful, if your thoughts are grim, your energy leaden, your feelings flush with self-pity: I suggest getting very, very curious about what element of reality you're denying, repressing, and hiding from.

Noticing Your Havingness Level

For the next week, I would like you to pay very close attention to your moods and the kinds of thoughts and perceptions that accompany them.

In my experience, certain kinds of moods bring with them certain kinds of thoughts and perceptions. When the mood changes, the thoughts and perceptions dramatically alter.

In this way, thoughts and emotions "chunk" together to form narrow tunnels of perception and state-dependent memory that can wildly distort reality for the worse.

I want you to begin to get sensitive to your own habits of distortion.

Specifically, I would like you to notice when you feel some flavor of "good"—close, connected, energized happy, hopeful, prosperous, etc., . . .

. . . and then to also notice exactly how long you are willing to tolerate feeling good before you start to turn yourself off with worrying, doubting, getting offended.

Here's an example:

Let's say you have dinner with a friend and it's a lovely time.

You have a great conversation, you laugh until you cry, you eat tasty food, and you feel good.

You've experienced connection, closeness, joviality, and pleasure.

Then dinner concludes, you wish your friend a goodnight, and you head home.

As you get into your car to return to your house, your heart feels warm and you notice that your thoughts about tomorrow are optimistic, and that you have some ideas bubbling up for a project you're working on.

How long does your good mood last?

Are you still in a wonderful mood when you get home?

Or somewhere during the journey does your mind fixate on some detail your friend mentioned about another person you both know who just got the kind of career boon you'd like to have?

Do you start feeling down on yourself and envious as you think about this mutual acquaintance?

Do you start worrying about how maybe you're not really as good at what you do as you should be, and thinking about how your retirement account is a bit sparse, and what are you going to do when your parents get old and need nurses, and what if . . .?

Do you turn yourself off with these kinds of thought patterns so you don't have to feel your good feelings anymore?

Notice whenever you feel good and notice when you turn yourself off, and exactly how you turn yourself off.

What's your favorite mode of turning yourself off? Is it worry about the future?

Or maybe doubting your own value and capability? Regretting a past mistake? Or saying something snippy to your partner to start an argument?

How exactly do you turn yourself off? How often?

Your task is to become the world's foremost expert on this subject, and to record your thoughts and reflections on the subject in your Magical Diary.

When you do the work of paying attention to how you turn yourself off, you are shifting your focus from the content (the situations, emotions, thoughts, "problems") of your life's experience to the previously unconscious, subtle processes that shape that content.

And as it happens, when you are more focused on the how (the subtle processes) of your experience rather than on the what (the content), you are getting closer to knowing yourself as the divine Self (the total context, the field of awareness), the ultimate Who.

It's a very large leap to go straight from knowing yourself as content (ego, personality, body, thoughts, feelings) to knowing yourself as context (pure presence, sat-chit-ananda, Pistis-Aletheia-Eros). So to make that leap more do-able, we are first getting acquainted with what's one step below the content—the processes.

When you get very intimate with how subtle (previously unconscious) processes shape the content of your experience, you are much less able to be "taken in" by that content, especially by painful dramas and limited perceptions of yourself (and the world and others) that once seemed so real and so pressing.

Instead, you see more and more how radically arbitrary the content in your experience is.

You gradually stop "taking it personally"—your heart becomes light as a feather (the prerequisite to a heavenly afterlife, according to ancient Egyptians, who knew a thing or two about magic) and with this lightness of heart comes a freedom to act decisively and to receive lavishly.

To continue with our noticing—I would also like you to get curious:

What if you just kept feeling really, really good for a whole week? Why not?

"Well, you see, I have realistic things to worry about. If I'm not worried and doubting myself and feeling somehow lacking, then I'm not in touch with reality."

Hmmmmmmm.

What if worrying and doubting yourself and feeling lacking were just the tools that you use to distract yourself from the work of living centered within the high sensation and high energy of the bliss that is your inherent nature?

Can you see a way that all the things you're worried about would rather easily resolve themselves if only you didn't turn yourself off?

- If you stayed feeling turned on, good, in high sensation and high energy—then you'd easily be able to be a force of nature in your work.

- Your creativity would flow, your social energy would flow.

- You'd network and exchange with others, your status would rise.

- Inspirations and ideas would come to you that just can't come to you when you're turned off.

- You'd have the energy to act on those inspirations, you'd make something awesome, and you'd feel confident about it's value.

- As you confidently, relentlessly sold your inspired awesomeness to the world (as a service, product, art, whatever), your income would increase, and your retirement account and the care of your aging parents would no longer be a problem.

This is just one small example of how learning to stay centered and grounded in turned-on, high sensation, and high energy (from now on we'll just say "turn-on") is actually the most responsible, beneficial, in-touch-with-reality thing you can do.

You'll always be more productive, energetic, connectable, and inspired in a turned-on state than a turned-off state.

So why do we turn ourselves off, ever?

Well, the short answer is that we have a weird, funny kink for that kind of thing.

We turn ourselves off because we actually just really like it in a secret, freaky way.

The good news is that it's possible to get turned on about being turned off. I know that sounds weird—but you can be:

Angry and turned on about it

Sad and turned on about it

Tired and turned on about it

Defeated and turned on about it

Grieving and turned on about it

Disgusted and turned on about it

Scared and turned on about it

Self-pitying and turned on about it

. . . you can be "the turned-on version" of anything.

To be "turned on" about any feeling state, including feeling any variation of "turned off," just means to be in total, unreserved approval of that state.

When you're in total, turned-on approval of your state, you're deciding to see that state as a way that you are "good for yourself" rather than as a way that you are "bad for yourself."

So rather than resenting that something made you angry, try getting excited that you're angry.

Rather than thinking you shouldn't be sad, try celebrating the tender exaltation of your sadness.

Instead of being annoyed with yourself for being so self-pitying, give the most fan-girl level of approval you are capable of giving to your self-pity—the kind of approval that you might normally reserve only for your favorite musician or movie star.

I'm saying: Adopt an aesthetic rather than a moral attitude to your feeling states.

In doing this, you practice being the artist of your life rather than the judge of it.

As an experiment, the next time you feel funky, rather than judging how you feel, just savor it as if it was a virtual reality experience crafted for you by the world's foremost artist.

The world's foremost artist is actually you, but for the sake of our thought experiment let's distance ourselves a bit—in fact, let's say a lady who just won the Venice Biennale for her brilliant installation art has just designed this virtual reality "I'm a failure" feeling (or whatever) for you.

Can you savor the failure feeling's nuances? Taste its pungent and grassy notes? Cherish its silky-yet-grainy texture?

Get excited about what an exquisite take on the "I'm a failure" theme it represents for this new season, drawing on a bold fresh palette of "I still don't know what I'm doing with my life"?

Practice liking that you're feeling what you're feeling.

Practice liking that you like what you like to feel.

I know that sounds a bit silly, but most of us habitually practice not liking that we like what we like to feel.

Why not try it the other way around?

How to Feel Your Real Feelings (Not Your Fake Ones)

Sigmund Freud has gone out of style in recent years, with fair reason. His rather convoluted theories about childhood development, for example, had more to do with his own hang-ups and the politics of 19th-century Vienna than with universal truths.

However, Freud did have some profound insights about the defense mechanisms that we humans use to protect our egos from uncomfortable unconscious facts. These insights are babies that shouldn't be thrown out with the Oedipal bathwater.

Among the defense mechanisms that Freud spotted, perhaps most relevant to our current work is one very tricky flip called reaction formation.

In essence, a reaction formation occurs when a situation stimulates a forbidden feeling, so before you can become consciously aware of that forbidden feeling, your ego stages an over-the-top performance of an emotion which is opposite to the forbidden feeling, as a way of hiding the forbidden feeling both from you and from other people.

A classic example of a reaction formation would be a high school jock who feels and acts disgusted whenever he sees a feminine gay guy—the disgust may be strongly felt, but it is still an over-the-top performance designed by the jock's ego to keep out of awareness his own feelings of homosexual attraction to the feminine gay guy.

Less obvious examples of reaction formation might include:

- Feeling wildly offended at the slightest slight
(A way to cover up awareness of masochistic desire to receive insult)

- Feeling tremendously guilty when you've disappointed someone
  (A way to cover up awareness of sadistic desire to inflict pain)

- Feeling very anxious in social situations
  (A way to cover up feelings of budding connection and intimacy, and also vicious aggression—usually both)

- Feeling massively annoyed and put-upon by family
  (A way to cover up vulnerable feelings of love and gratitude)

The thing about reaction formations is that they are *reactions*, and not responses to life.

Genuine responsive emotions have an open, connecting, "moving" quality to them. They feel fresh and spontaneous including "dark" genuine emotions like anger and grief.

Reacting, covering-something-up emotions have a hard, closed, robotic, repetitive quality to them.

Over time you can begin to notice the difference and be able to directly feel when you're in a compulsive reaction formation rather than a genuine emotional response.

The funny thing about reaction formations is that they are very, very good at repressing our awareness of our identity with the divine spark—the happy holy whore in all of us that happens to enjoy everything, including all the "fucked-up stuff" that we consciously disapprove of mightily.

In other words, at a fundamental level, we have all these reaction formations to hide our own saintliness, our own willingness to experience everything with total love.

The most repressed item in your unconscious is your own total grace.

Of all the things to be embarrassed about, the ego is most embarrassed by your total grace, and so it puts on a show (with reaction formations) to convince you that there are elements of your instinctual, animal nature (like sadomasochistic pleasure, or homosexual attraction, or incestuous attraction, or the urge to destroy and decimate) that you can't accept.

But it's just not true—you *can* experience anything with total grace, and your total grace can transmute the most gruesome brutality into shining presence.

The thing about the ego is that it needs a sense of opposition, of refusal, of rejection in order to maintain itself. It has to say: "No! That is awful! I don't like that! No, that's not me!" to something in order to define itself as separate from the undulating whole of the weird fractal hologram of life.

Which is great, of course, and it's a wise game to play in many childhood survival situations; it's just not ultimately true, and it can become a limiting burden in adulthood because the divinity that we essentially are rejects nothing, refuses nothing, even extreme experiences of pain.

In fact, according to some of the most touching myths we have, the divine often actively seeks out extreme experiences of pain in order to show off how divinely accepting it is.

Odin, for example, put out his right eye and hung from a tree for nine days in order to gain knowledge of the mysteries.

Yet, just because the divine in you enjoys or feels pleasure or attraction to someone or something doesn't mean you automatically have to pursue it.

Think back to our high school jock. Let's say he realizes that his over-the-top disgust for feminine gay guys he meets is a reaction formation, one that's covering up some scary feelings of attraction. He could just let those feelings of attraction exist in his body—noticing them, not judging them, not rejecting them.

He doesn't have to act on those feelings of attraction if he doesn't think it's the best idea for him and he doesn't have to convulse with disgust and act like a bully to hide those feelings.

So if you realize that your over-the-top guilt when you disappoint someone is a cover-up for a twinge of sadistic glee, it doesn't mean you have to go on a rampage trying to torture your friends and family with disappointment.

It just means you can let the ripple of glee arise in your body, feel it without judging it, and stay centered and present with the flow of life instead of throwing yourself into a stinky pool of reactive guilt.

If we all allow ourselves to feel the unconscious, divine, kinky pleasure we've been suppressing, then we are left with just our intelligence to guide our decisions, and that's great. Your own intelligence and consciously chosen principles are a much better ethical compass than your reactive feelings of guilt.

How to Not Take Yourself So Seriously

The next time you notice yourself feeling guilty or resentful in the course of your day (hint: it's usually a sticky, stinky combination of both that's otherwise known as "feeling bad" or "feelin' some kinda way")—try this:

Take a moment and imagine as strongly and as vividly that you can that there is a very loud, very colorful chorus of utterly fabulous, silly, adorable, over-the-top cheerleaders celebrating your guilty resentful yuck.

They're dancing, they're shaking their butts, they're shaking their pom-poms, they're jumping up and down, trying to do splits and failing at it, jumping back up and grinning.

They're splashing rainbow glitter paint around. Maybe they're all drag queens, maybe they're all roly-poly pink elephants, maybe they're all your best friends in super-goofy sequined outfits. They're chanting,

"How do we want to feel? LACKING AND WRONG!"

"When do we want to feel it? NOW!"

"WOOOOOO-HOOOO! FUCK YEAH! Go Team Wrong and Bad! Go Go GO!"

Just visualizing this can be great; it's even better if you also join in and start jumping up and down and shaking what your mama gave you along with your imaginary pom-poms.

"We're injured! We're hurt! We're wounded!"

"We suck! THEY SUCK! We suck so much! They suck *worse*!"

"nah-NAH-nah-HEY-hey HEY life SUCKS!"

"YEAAAAAAAAAAAHHHHHHHHHHHH!!!!"

You get the idea. You can add in your favorite pop songs and comedians. I like Queen's "We Will Rock You." Make your cheerleading team as nutty and funny and loud and catchy as you can. Work on your butt-shakes, seeking maximum sass. Whatever you do, do not be content with less than maximum butt-shake sass.

The more you do this, the more you associate feeling bad / wrong/resentful with hilarious, sexy quirky silliness, which—wait for it—is its true nature.

After practicing The Cheerleaders for a good while, you'll eventually feel the twitches of a guilt trip or a blame session coming on and you'll automatically find it funny.

By the way, this is a very deep and super-serious mystical teaching.

Why? Because as Dante well knew, the most useful way to perceive life is *as a divine comedy*.

I mean, you can perceive it as a tragedy, but you might find that you're too busy crying to get anything done or help anyone else. When you perceive life as a comedy, you receive rich infusions of energy that give you the strength to move mountains.

Practice The Cheerleaders avidly for a week. Write about what you notice in your journal.

How to Feel Good in Your Body

Let's say that you're in bodily pain of some kind right now. Or, sometimes even more perplexing, let's say you're in some type of emotional pain *about* your body. Maybe you don't like how your body looks or you're frustrated about aging.

This issue of bodily maintenance and the task of feeling good about our bodies is one of the distinctly annoying parts of incarnation, perhaps because our bodies (like everything else) are always changing, always a minute older and more "vintage" than they used to be. They're also always with us. Hard to avoid.

A big invitation that I want to extend to you here is to come to take this pain (whether physical or emotional) way less personally. To come to relate to your pain (whether in or about your body) as "the pain" rather than "my pain."

It's "the pain" simply because no matter how terrible it is, other people have felt it, and are feeling it. Right now. Down the block and all over the world. And while that's a bit sobering to think about, it's also beautiful.

Pain becomes suffering when we take it personally, as if it reflects something uniquely meaningful (and bad) about us. And of course it does—it reflects that we're willing to take pain personally. Haha!

The more we do that, the more we suffer, and suffering has a remarkable way of generating more pain to suffer about. The cycle of bodily pain generating suffering, which sparks more pain, is another one of those seemingly seamless loops.

The way to interrupt the loop is to practice experiencing the pain impersonally.

One very useful means to learn how to experience pain impersonally is called Tonglen meditation.

Tonglen comes to us from Tibetan Buddhism. The current Dalai Lama has remarked that Tonglen is the most powerful tantric practice that there is. You might think that having sex while imagining yourself and your partner to be eight-armed luminous, fire-breathing deities would be the most powerful tantric practice that there is, but nope, the Dalai Lama says it's Tonglen.

Tonglen means "taking and sending." It's a practice of taking in the pain of other people and sending out happiness, good fortune, and good wishes. It is a tantric practice because tantra is all about the transformation of energy. In this way, tantra is identical with alchemy. "Alchemy" is pretty much just the Western esoteric word for what's called "tantra" in Eastern traditions.

Tonglen transforms the energy of pain and suffering into the energy of compassion, togetherness, and love. There are many different sets of Tonglen instructions out in the world. The Shambhala teacher Pema Chodron has a wonderful set that you can easily find online. Here's my version:

Tonglen Meditation

Notice the pain that you're feeling. It could be a specific pain somewhere in your body, or it could be an emotional pain that comes from judging your body as "not good enough" in some way.

Take a moment to imagine all the millions of people in the world who are currently feeling exactly the same way that you are right now.

There are millions of people with fibromyalgia, millions with acid reflux, or with an ache in their shoulders. Millions who feel shame and guilt about the shape and size of their bodies. Bring these people who share your particular affliction to mind.

Decide that you're heroically willing to experience all the pain and suffering of these others. Decide that you're infinitely, courageously willing to experience the total sensation, without an ounce of reservation or holding back.

Inhale slowly. Imagine that as you breathe in, you're breathing in a thick, cold, heavy smoke filled with all the pain of "this ache" or "this shame" that's experienced by millions of people around the world and down your block who are suffering with the same suffering that you have.

You're breathing in the pain and experiencing it fully on their behalf, so they don't have to.

You are dropping all your resistance, all your resentment, all your refusal of this pain and instead you are opening your heart fully to it.

Hold your breath for a few moments. Imagine as you hold your breath that the cold, acrid smoke dissolves a brittle shell around your heart. Now, with its brittle shell dissolved by the pain of others, your heart is tender and exposed and shining a gold light.

Imagine that the gold light transforms and purifies the cold black smoke of pain that you've just breathed in.

Exhale slowly. As you exhale, imagine a warm golden healing light pouring out from your heart, riding your breath, and touching all the other people in the world who feel the same pain and suffering in their bodies that you do.

Breathe normally for a few minutes while you visualize people in your neighborhood and around the world being healed, and warmed and made happy by the golden light emanating from your bare heart.

After a few minutes of seeing everyone who shares your affliction freed of it, again take in a deep breath of thick cold black smoke, full of the pain that you feel and that others feel.

Again, pause your breath for a moment as you visualize the thick black smoke being heated, purified, and transformed into golden light by the electricity of your bare, tender heart.

Again, breathe out the hot healing, golden light to everyone else who suffers from the same affliction as you.

Again, observe all of these people being even more healed and being made even more happy by this golden light that your heart willingly radiates to them.

Rinse, repeat.

For a single session of Tonglen, aim to do ten taking-and-sending breaths, giving yourself ample time between taking-and-sending breaths to breathe normally while you visualize the healing of others.

You might notice that after a week of practicing Tonglen, you begin to feel a deep, soft sense of connection every time your painful affliction comes to your attention. This deep, soft sense of connection can help you feel more at peace with your own affliction. Instead of your pain making you feel isolated from other people, you now know how to use it to make yourself feel more connected with them.

Tonglen is a great support practice for shadow integration work and is actually similar to EK—the key practice outlined in this book—in that it invites you to take the courageous step of feeling the pain fully and bravely, with good humor and kindness, without resistance or resentment, fear or shame, as a heroic act on behalf of all other beings who have the same pain.

You might ask yourself, "Does Tonglen actually heal other people? Am I lying to myself when I'm visualizing other people being healed by my breathing out golden light?"

The answer to this is, your practice of Tonglen heals *you*, and the more you are healed, the more healing you will notice in other people around you. Only healing can recognize healing—as within, so without.

So yes, in a roundabout way, it does. The more you practice Tonglen, the more you come to experience pain and suffering as "*the* pain and suffering" rather than "*my* pain and suffering which proves that I am uniquely wrong, bad, and unworthy."

When pain and suffering are thought of as universal, and not personal, they can no longer prove that you are uniquely deserving of them.

In other words, you come to realize that you're not and you never have been uniquely terrible or wonderful. Instead, you're a "a garden variety human" just like "a garden variety cabbage."

This can sound a little sad, like maybe you won't be special anymore. But paradoxically, your *real* power, your *real* specialness, your *actual* ability to influence and help others, rests in you ever-more-deeply understanding and enjoying your "garden variety-ness."

The word "individuate" comes from a Latin term which means "impossible to divide" ("in" = "not" and "dividuate" = divided; thus—"individuated" means "unable to be divided"). In other words, to individuate means to become whole. Whole with what? Whole with everything.

The more "individuated" you are, the more you have understood yourself as a unity (with all other humans and all other everything), a unity which is impossible to divide.

A bit of a mind fuck, huh? And here you thought "individual" meant "unique"! Well, it doesn't. It means "indivisible." But the weird thing is—(and everything that has to do with magic is weird, queer, nondual, and multivalent, if you haven't noticed already)— the unity and the "garden-variety-ness" of humanity has a distinct way that it wants to express itself through you. That distinction is your "individuality."

As the great modernist dancer Martha Graham remarked, "There is a vitality, a life force, an energy, a quickening that is translated through you into action, and because there is only one of you in all time, this expression is unique. And if you block it, it will never exist through any other medium and will be lost."

The most common way that we block the rare quickening that we are is by worrying that our pain and suffering mean that we're uniquely terrible or uniquely cursed (in other words—feeling guilty or resentful about it).

Because the Law of Attraction teaches "you get what you think about," sometimes people get worried that by heroically being willing to take on the pain and suffering of all other people who have their same affliction they will be bringing more of that affliction upon themselves. That's just not how it works.

By being heroically (heroine-ly) willing to take on the pain and suffering of all other people who have your same affliction, you give yourself a damn good reason to open to fully feeling, without resentment or resistance or hold-back or reservation of any kind, the physical and emotional sensation is already present for you.

At an ultimate level, you *are* "all the others," inescapably.

Don't no one get liberated 'less we all get liberated, 'cause liberation is something that consciousness will spontaneously project everywhere, just like it can spontaneously project "bad-ness," "wrongness," and "not-enoughness" everywhere.

In Buddhism, bodishattvas take a vow that they won't leave the Wheel of Incarnation in Samsara (the world as we know it, with all its fucked-up stuff) until all beings are liberated. But the great cosmic joke is that it's impossible to leave the Wheel of Samsara. As the Heart Sutra will tell you, Samsara is Nirvana, Heaven, release from suffering. Nirvana is Samsara. Earth is Heaven and Hell. The jewel is in the lotus. The lotus is in the jewel.

Om mani padme hum, om gate gate paragate, parasamgate, bodhi svha, forever and ever, amen, praise to Allah, hail Hecate, thanks to Ganesha, high-five to Baphomet, big kisses to and from your Holy Guardian Angel.

Being fully willing to feel what's already present without contracting, without tensing into aversion (resentment) to avoid it—that is an exercise of your own deep divine power and sovereignty, that is the loving willingness that transforms, that transmutes.

In Law of Attraction terms, Tonglen gives you a very heroic, "high" vibration, actually.

And this loving-willingness to feel pain without avoiding or contracting is the Philosopher's Stone, the Diamond Body, the secret indestructible, indivisible substance that changes the cold lead of shitty life experience into sparkly hot gold.

Tonglen is a form of compassion cultivation. Compassion means "to feel with" or "to experience with." Compassion isn't pity; it isn't trying to protect or save people from the consequences of their choices.

Compassion is a condition of letting yourself joyfully, vulnerably, sensationally feel "all the things" of life with the knowing that everything you feel, you feel with.

It's actually impossible to feel not-with, to feel alone—but still the illusion that we can suffer alone is a persistent one, and Tonglen dissolves it.

How to Stop Sucking at Love

It is a truth universally acknowledged that most of us suck at love, at least a little bit.

What is less universally acknowledged is that our partners (or lack of partners) are *always exactly as we unconsciously wish them to be*. You knew I was going to say that, didn't you?

Out there in the cosmic ethers I can just hear a full chorus of:

"Oh, no, Carolyn, you don't understand—my partner (or my ex) does XYZ awful things that definitely no part of me *ever* would want them to do."

Ah, but you see, I *do* understand, precisely. And I want you to fully and precisely understand this point too, because once you do, a door opens up for you to have immensely fulfilling relationships.

You can integrate and evolve those previously unconscious desires of yours for a partner who cheats, mopes, drinks, fails to wash dishes, or believes in Flat Earth theories—whatever your particular kink amongst the thousands possible happens to be.

At such a point of recognition and integration, you either lose all interest in the present relationship and end it gracefully, freeing yourself to go find a better one, or you find that you, yourself, your partner, and the relationship as a whole, evolve in a fascinating way.

Sound good? Excellent.

Here's a tale about how I came to realize this less-than-universally-acknowledged truth in my own experience, and then we'll get into discussing fruitful means of exploring it in your own experience. Years ago, as I started to make a lot more money after my initial discovery of Existential Kink, I became curious if the kinky approach could likewise help me with my jacked-up love life. At the time, I was in a physically abusive relationship with a jealous, controlling guy. Remember the guy I told you I met through a Craig's List personals ad—because I was having such a tough time finding someone to date? To refresh your memory, he was controlling and violent. Our relationship was tumultous, dramatic, and dangerous.

And yet, after much inquiry and reflection, I realized I actually *loved* how controlling and violent he was. Loved, loved, *loved* it. I adored the feeling of being important that came from having this guy treat me like I was a supply of heroin that he had to manage in order to have it available at all times.

When we were in the throes of a fight, I could savor the breath-held, dizzying sensation of deep constriction.

I could use him and his emotional dysfunction to keep me contained, so that I didn't have to risk exploring myself or the world without him.

Part of what kept me hooked into the relationship was the profound joy of resenting him and his controlling violence. Another part of what kept me hooked in was the feeling that I could only have this terrible relationship because *I* was terrible, so if I could just become un-terrible, then I could leave him.

But as long as I was terrible, I reasoned, I might as well stay with him, because even though he's possessive and violent, he's more entertaining than being alone.

So I tried to become an un-terrible person, but that didn't work. The very act of trying to be un-terrible generally makes one more certain that one is terrible.

I adored using the constriction of a relationship with a jealous, controlling guy to keep me contained because I didn't want to face the great unknown.

I was bound to him. I was in a self-inflicted state of bondage.
Bondage?
Me, into bondage?

I looked up Japanese rope bondage online and realized that the experience of being tightly, elaborately bound is something that can feel exquisite, and for which some people pay a lot of money.

And which I was generously, metaphorically giving to myself for free.

When it finally occurred to me that the logic of "I can only get this terrible relationship because I am terrible" was not true, I realized the following: "I have this terrible relationship because my unconscious is just *that* kinky and really, secretly likes feeling maniacally controlled by an evil outside agency." This was *much* more true. And when I discovered this truth, a giant space opened up in my body.

I practiced The Basic Existential Kink Meditation as I described it to you in Lesson 3.

I allowed myself to consciously feel the previously unconscious pleasure I felt in being violently controlled. I breathed it in deeply and fully, so that it shook and saturated me. Tidal waves of electric current rocked me. I *got off* on it.

After that, I could no longer hate and resent the guy for being a controlling, violent jerk. And without that luscious glue of resentment, the relationship was just no longer interesting.

I wished him well, he threw some stuff at me, and then I got on a plane for Indonesia. As I sat alone in my apartment in Ubud, Bali, which is indeed a *very* nice place to ponder one's singleness (thanks for the tip, Elizabeth Gilbert), I realized I *also* had an unconscious, repressed, secret desire to avoid real, intimate relationships that might truly grow and change me.

For a long time I had thought it was just my cruel fate to lose at love. I thought it was fate every time I got rejected or wound up with some controlling jerk, but I finally acknowledged that a shadowy part of me was actually getting deeply fulfilled.

I realized that it was not really fate (some outside agency) that determined my experience—it was *me*, my own intense desires that conflicted with what my ego thought I wanted, and so I had disowned them.

I learned that in order to enjoy this fulfillment, all I had to do was accept the beautiful humiliation of it.

Fulfillment is always humiliating, because it never happens within the bounds our conscious ego prescribes for it.

The word "humiliation" is an interesting one. It comes from the Latin word *hummus*—meaning the ground, the dirt—so to be humiliated is essentially to be brought down to earth. To be brought down to earth feels embarrassing because it means our high-flying fantasies of alienation have been punctured.

I realized, after accepting a lot of wondrous humiliation, that my ego, in fact, *cannot ever be fulfilled* because it's precisely an illusion of separation, of lack, of being independent and apart from the totality.

Only my *whole* being can be fulfilled, and the wholeness of my being tends to want stuff that counterbalances my ego's straightforward desires for the "good stuff."

My whole being (perverse shadow desires and all) is inevitably, invariably being fulfilled at each and every moment. It's only a matter of whether or not I am willing to set aside my attachment to my conscious mind's *tsk-tsk* judgment long enough to enjoy the massive fulfillment that's always-already present in all the ways life seems to be "torturing" me.

After spending time in Indonesia savoring the deep dark fulfillment of my "tragic" (to my ego) single-hood, I discovered that the hungry shadow in me was satisfied, and that I was actually ready to accept a loving partner into my life. Specifically, I learned to get off on feeling rejected, unwanted, locked-out-of-Paradise. That "rejected" feeling was so sweet that I gave it to myself every day. It was mesmerizing, fascinating, compelling as all great fictions are.

Eventually, after practicing Existential Kink on the harrowing, irresistible sensation of rejection that my single-hood (and unrequited loves) afforded me, a fountain of joy would spring up in my heart whenever I even thought about being rejected. Not long after that, I got together with the wonderful, hot, hilarious man who's now my husband.

Of course, the fairy tale doesn't end there.

Healing often happens in layers. I had healed myself enough to accept intimacy with a great match, but not yet enough to totally allow myself to perpetually enjoy that intimacy. In the whirlwind that is new love, I let myself forget about my joy-in-rejection.

I reasoned I would never have to deal with that sad 'ole single stuff again. So I decided that I was once again someone who didn't like to be rejected. Thus, even after getting together with the marvelous love of my life, I still would find ways to to feel fictionally rejected within the relationship, particularly if he spoke to me in a sassy tone of voice.

Yes, that's all it would take to send me into a despairing huff. A sassy tone of voice. Clearly, my kinkiness was really grasping for crumbs at this stage. That's when I had to learn to apply, at a whole new level, the less-than-universally-acknowledged-truth that my partner was showing up exactly as a shadowy part of me wanted him to. I realized that every time I felt upset at one of these perceived "rejections," my feeling of upset didn't have the soft, flowing, open quality of genuine grief. Instead my upset felt hard and stuck and repetitive.

Indeed: the lady doth protest too much.

The offense I took at his sassy tone was a reaction formation, a shallow show of protest to keep my deep unconscious joy and desire for rejection disguised from my conscious awareness [see

Exercise 7: How to Feel Your Real Feelings (Not Your Fake Ones) for more discussion of reaction formations].

As Freud pointed out, when humans are turned on by something that their conscious mind doesn't deem acceptable, they will block that turn-on from their own awareness by automatically covering it up with a display of offense and disgust. In remembering and giving more permission to my joy in the sensation of rejection, I learned that I actually find sassiness really hot. My man is still sassy, and I'm happier than ever.

Okay, so there's *my* story; now let's talk about yours.

I invite you to do Inquiry, Deepest Fear Inventory, and Existential Kink practices on any issues that may be coming up in your love life.

I also want to invite you to take full, unflinching, complete and total responsibility for how not just *you*, but for how *your partner* shows up in relationship.

And just because you take complete and total responsibility for how they show up, this does not mean that you need to stay with them forever or even for a single additional minute.

It just means that you're being radically honest about how experience actually works.

"But Carolyn, aren't I supposed to just take responsibility for my own side of things? How can I take responsibility for another person's part?"

Because that other person whom you are in a relationship with is a fractal holograph of you, one whom you can only ever experience through *your own subjective awareness*. Really take that in. Let it sink into your noggin. There is no way that you can ever "objectively" experience another person.

You can have perceptions of your partner and then inquire of your friends and family about *their* perceptions of your partner, and thus try to get a more well-rounded "objective" view of the situation . . . but still, *all other people,* including your friends and family, are *only ever* experienced in your own subjective awareness, and your awareness has a filter that is heavily colored by your deepest unconscious beliefs and desires.

You can come up with "proof" that other people exist outside your subjective awareness by referring to photographs and videos and stories about them from other people—*and still, every shred of this proof can only ever be experienced in your own subjective awareness.*

I'm not saying that other people don't exist, or arguing for solipsism. My stance is that we are all distinct and equally "real" characters in a shared dream being dreamt by divinity that we call "material reality."

We are all in fact not really limited little characters, but rather we are all this dreaming divinity, just as every character in your nighttime dream is in reality, *you.*

So what I *am* saying is is that your dream-character's quality of awareness in this material plane has a hell of a lot to do with how the other characters in this waking-life dream will appear to you. The old saying is quite true: all other people are our mirrors. They reflect to us qualities in our selves that we love or loathe. It's a cliche because it's an uncomfortable, inescapable fact. We humans are microcosms of the macrocosm, which means we each contain *everything, every* possible quality.

The people to whom you are attracted enough to get into any kind of more-than-a-weekend relationship with are especially, terrifyingly accurate mirrors.

Consider this: a little-understood quirk of consciousness is that whenever we perceive a quality "somewhere," we will end up perceiving it "everywhere."

So when we perceive ourselves in an unhappy fashion, it is a guarantee that we will eventually unconsciously project that same perception of "badness" or "wrongness" onto our loved ones and (again, unconsciously) invite them to project that same "badness" or "wrongness" onto us. This is what one might call a vicious circle. The unconscious creative power of our perception and belief generates a seamless feedback loop that appears to be "objective reality" when actually it's an appearance called forth by our level of consciousness.

The way to interrupt this feedback loop is to take total responsibility for the way that *all other beings* show up in relation to us. When we do this, we are forced to examine and integrate the disowned qualities and desires in our own selves. John Demartini outlines an excellent means of doing this kind of integration in his book *The Breakthrough Experience*, which I hope you will investigate.

Demartini's *Breakthrough Experience* process is very thorough. You take an influential person in your life (say, your mom or your husband) and make lists of every quality you enjoy and don't enjoy about them, then make a list of at least a handful of other people who would say that you have *the exact same quality to the exact same degree*.

Then, you write about how the other person having the not-enjoyed qualities has actually benefitted you, and about how you having the same not-enjoyed qualities have benefitted others, then write about how the other person's enjoyed qualities have actually harmed you, and how your having the enjoyed qualities has harmed others. Whew.

After doing work like that, it's miraculously impossible to maintain self-righteousness. In doing this kind of examination of how the other people in our lives reflect qualities in our own selves, we thereby take the unconscious creative power of our perception and belief, and begin to make it conscious.

I know that I belabor this point a bit, but just think for a moment about how much vast power you are forfeiting every second that you refuse to take total responsibility for the way that your currently unconscious stuff is generating your world and relationships.

The Parable of the Six Kinds of Beings

There's a Buddhist parable that describes the generative, fictional function of awareness quite well. Here's how the 17th century Tibetan monk Ngawang Kunga Tenzin explained the parable:

> Ultimately there is nothing other than mind alone; nevertheless, because of delusion and karma it manifests as all kinds of things. This is similar to the different perceptions of water by the six kinds of beings. Water is indeed only one thing, but if the six kinds of beings were together at a river bank, when looking at it they would see it in different ways.
>
> A being of a hot hell would see a river of fire, while one from a cold hell would see it as snow and ice. For the hungry ghosts known as pretas it would be pus and blood. Animals who live underwater would see it as their abode, while those scattered on land would see it as drink. Humans would also see it as drink, and accordingly they would classify it into drinking or non-drinking water.
>
> The demigods called asuras would perceive it as weaponry. Gods would see it as nectar (amrita). So beings would see what we perceive as water in different ways according to their particular karmic perception and thus water becomes manifold. This is known as the karmic perception of one's mind. Ultimately things do not exist outside—they are only projections of the mind.
>
> —from *The Royal Seal of Mahamudra, Volume One, A Guidebook for the Realization of Co-emergence*

We can consider the "six kinds of beings" of Buddhist lore to be potentially literal and also to be metaphors for levels of consciousness that we might inhabit throughout our lives or throughout our day, or in a given arena of experience.

Hungry Ghosts in Love

Of course a hungry ghost doesn't consciously think he *wants* to see the river as pus and blood; he's painfully thirsty and believes that he would much rather have a river of water in front of him, but a hungry ghost is totally possessed by unconscious demands, lacks human awareness, and simply can't see the drink that's there.

Many of us are like hungry ghosts in love.

There are loving and lovable beings all around us (maybe already living with us!) but sometimes we struggle to see their thirst-slaking wonders because we're too stuck in our habitual grooves of perception.

In other words, we might see our partners or potential partners as depriving us of some fulfillment that we want, but the truth is that we're *the only ones* with any agency whatsoever over the generative perception of our own awareness. We're *the only ones* who can trick ourselves into seeing a repulsive river of pus and blood where otherwise we might find clear-flowing water or even divine nectar.

Of course the same thing goes for our perception of our own selves. Do you see yourself as depriving or diminishing yourself somehow?

Do you believe your past actions or the condition of your body or the quality of your work or anything else about you limits you and leaves you hungry for fulfillment?

What if that perception was entirely fabricated? What if you were actually a wish-fulfilling gem, capable of generating magnificent satisfaction of all kinds at any moment?

The only way to find out is to work on adjusting your perception—and of course perception is shaped by our habitual (which is to say unconscious) attitude.

The most efficient way to adjust your perception is to make your previously unconscious process of perception conscious, in a gracious manner that celebrates the fulfillment already present, thus implanting an attitude of celebration and fulfillment into your unconscious.

The basic Existential Kink practice as described in Part 1 does just that. Deepest Fear Inventory and Inquiry help maintain it.

A Hungry Ghost Transformed by Existential Kink

Imagine that our aforementioned hungry ghost on the riverbank—by some unexpected blessing of a great bodhisattva—gains the ability to at least temporarily set aside his all-consuming worry about his gnawing hunger and instead he simply takes time to appreciate and enjoy the river of pus and blood surging along before him in all its stinking, hideous glory, knowing it to be the spectacular product of his own unconscious perception.

The hungry ghost sits on the riverbank, struck with pleasure and awe at the sheer, revolting power of his mind, genuinely, un-ironically celebrating the stinking river of pus and blood for what it actually is: an impressive satisfaction of his own previously unconscious creativity. He enjoys the wonder of it so much that for a moment he forgets his obsession with his hunger, with his pain, and simply feels filled with the marvel of creation.

Well, if the hungry ghost were to do this, he would rapidly become human. His perception would change and he would see lovely, drinkable water.

Why? Because as long as the hungry ghost believes that only the deprivation he already perceives is real, *he will continue to perceive only deprivation*. That's the vicious circle.

Likewise, as long as you believe that only the deprivation of rich fulfillment that you perceive in your love life is real, *you will continue to perceive only deprivation.*

You will experience your partner as "lacking" in some way. Or, you'll perceive yourself as "lacking" a partner altogether. But the minute the hungry ghost gains enough awareness to see that in truth, a mechanism of ever-present, seamless, circular, self-confirming fulfillment is at work, then he perceives that fulfillment is actually much more real than deprivation.

After all, deprivation was what he believed was there, but it was the ever-present, self-confirming mechanism of fulfillment *that fulfilled his perception of deprivation!* Once the hungry ghost perceives that fulfillment is more real than deprivation, he can start to perceive fulfillment everywhere because if we perceive something *somewhere,* we will eventually perceive it *everywhere.* That's the quirk of consciousness.

The hungry ghost can now start to perceive the river as water that can fulfill his thirst, and with this transmutation wrought by his consciousness, he becomes human.

As a human, this character is even more lucky because he now has the awareness and freedom to deliberately practice expanding his perception of the reality of fulfillment to include everything. He can work his way up to perceiving the world as total perfection.

This is the Great Work, the attainment of the Mahamudra. This is how we turn water into wine. Or nectar.

Whatever you prefer.

How to Stop Pretending You're Not Enlightened Already

"One does not become enlightened by imagining figures of light, but by making the darkness conscious," our old friend Jung liked to say.

As you know by now, I agree with him whole-heartedly on this point, and this is exactly what we have been working on throughout this book. While "making the darkness conscious" is an ongoing project, it's still fun to allow oneself to enjoy enlightenment right now.

You may be wondering, what does enlightenment have to do with "getting what you want," with "creating your own experience"? What does enlightenment have to do with magic?

The simple answer is that all magic leads to enlightenment, eventually.

Magic involves communicating with and integrating hidden truths of the unconscious in order to dissolve old ways of being and open up new possibilities, thereby discovering for yourself the daunting symmetry of the poetic analogy that shapes the world: "as above, so below; as within, so without."

Consider for a moment that the whole of the physical world and of your body within it is itself a dimension of the unconscious.

Yes, you are aware of the physical world, can perceive it with your senses, and in this sense it is "conscious," but how much deliberate, personal control do you have over the flow of the ocean's tides, or the flow of your own blood?

Are not these processes usually ones that seem to happen all by themselves, without you knowing the whys or the hows or the where-to-fores? In fact, one could say that the whys and hows and where-to-fores of the tides and of your blood are *unknown*, *un*-conscious, to a great degree, governed by forces outside personal choice.

Your blood flows while you're asleep, doesn't it? The tides roll in and out without asking you about their timing, yes? To "make the unconscious, conscious" involves becoming personally aware of just how nonpersonal and interdependent all experience is.

This "becoming-aware"-ness is also a process of re-membering, of discovering the whole of the world as your extended body, and of your soul as the soul of the world, the Anima Mundi.

But what exactly does this have to do with getting what you want? Great question.

Gods of magic are always trickster gods. You get what you want, but along the way, the "you" in the equation changes. And that's not a bad thing at all. Eventually you come to identify less and less as your small, embattled ego self and more and more as the Self that inhabits all reality, in all bodies, in all times and all places.

This is the process of enlightenment, so give a wry smile and let yourself savor it.

How to Stop Torturing Others by Truly Appreciating the Art of Torture

A common sticking point in Existential Kink practice comes when one tries to work on habits or behaviors that one sees as negatively affecting not only just oneself, but others as well. After all, we're spiritual, sensitive, growth-oriented people, and we don't want to hurt other people.

And yet.

If you allow your shame or guilt to prevent you from fully relishing and owning such a pattern, you're likely to just keep repeating it because the shadowy urges that drive it will remain repressed, and when repressed they have *much* more power to direct your behavior than they do when fully acknowledged and celebrated.

Here's a common example among spiritual, growth-oriented types: let's say you're always about a half an hour late to everything you commit to.

Now obviously, this has negative effects for you—it's embarrassing; you might risk losing jobs or relationships due to this habit.

But when you go to EK it, you start to notice that what lies underneath your compulsion to be late all the time is a shadowy desire to make other people wait, to put your needs ahead of theirs, to make yourself important.

"Oh how awful," you might say to yourself. "I can't get off on that," you might say to yourself, "if I did I would be a total sociopathic narcissist."

That's incorrect, though. While society sometimes carelessly refers to sociopathic, narcissistic behavior as "shameless," people with sociopathic narcissism are so burdened by neurotic shame that they can't empathically feel their impact on other people, or even feel their own authentic desire for connection.

Such lack of empathy is the *opposite* of real shamelessness (which is liberating and opening); rather it's caused by shame that's so overpowering it shuts one down and creates numbness.

When you "get off" on patterns that unpleasantly impact others, you are allowing yourself to fully feel, with genuine shamelessness, the sensations and the underlying human desires of a situation.

The desire to make others wait *is a desire for power.*

Similarly (to mention some other common patterns you may have), the desire to pick fights with your partner to get attention, the desire to troll people on social media, the desire to bad-mouth colleagues as a way of gaining leverage at work, are all sideways manifestations of a desire for power.

This desire for power, this desire to have an impact on the world around you and to be *significant,* is an immensely normal, lovely, garden-variety human desire. The fact that you have it doesn't make you uniquely evil; it makes you *just like the rest of us.*

Folks who don't humble themselves enough to accept that their lust for power is both completely wonderful and *utterly, unremarkably ordinary* tend to either hide and suppress it into "nice" personas thoroughly laced with passive-aggressive behavior (like always being late) or, to mix this basic drive with grandiose resentment and to give it extraneous justifications like, "I must rise to power so I can eliminate all the evil-doers! I will implement THE FINAL SOLUTION!"

Or, sometimes folks do both, and then one day they go on a deadly shooting spree after writing a manifesto about how they've been "such a nice guy" all their life, wrongly spurned by cruel women who now must be murdered to punish them.

All nonhumble reactions to the *human, all-too-human* thirst for power have the effect of warping that natural, beautiful drive into numbness that steamrolls over other people instead of inspiring and uplifting them like genuine, epic power can.

If you boldly claim and revel in your previously suppressed desire for power, allowing yourself to savor the intense secret pleasure of all the times you've "accidentally" inconvenienced or upset others, you will find this doesn't morph you into a murderous fascist.

Instead it gives you the opportunity to compassionately feel your connection to all us other "awful" humans out there who have *the exact same desire for power,* and it liberates your awareness and energy so that you can start finding energizing, gorgeous ways to make your power felt in the world rather than acting it out in sideways, resentful, passive-aggressive fashions.

One of the amazing insights that Tani Thole and Leslie Rogers of the Light/Dark Institute passed onto me is that sadism isn't necessarily the desire to inflict pain; it's the desire to inflict *sensation,* to make oneself *felt.*

So if you're working on dissolving a passive-aggressive pattern that negatively impacts you and others, I encourage you to consider all the ways that you hold yourself back from giving others *the exact sensations that it would truly please you to give them.*

For example, maybe you're late all the time (thus inflicting sensations of frustration on others) and this is a compensation because you never let yourself inflict the kind of sensations on others *that would be actually fun and inspiring to you to inflict*— like your sexiness or your gut-busting zany humor.

In this case, go ahead and get off on your lateness, and then sign up for burlesque dancing classes, or stand-up comedy classes.

Learn to stir up massive sensation in your audiences with your jaw-dropping moxie and style. Maybe the sensation you really lust to inflict *is* pain. In that case, join your local BDSM group and find consenting partners to flog.

Play a bigger, bolder game. Find a way to give sensation to others in *exactly the way that you really want to give it to them.* Let them feel your importance and significance in a manner that delights both you and them.

Make it into a fine art.

Consider the idea that all the best artists and the most inspiring leaders are masters of torture. They torture us by getting us to feel deep emotions, by exposing taboos, by leading us through almost-unbearable sensations of anticipation, surprise, and revelation.

Your problem is not that you torture others; it's that *you don't torture them exquisitely enough.* So stop shaming yourself for torturing us, get off on all the sensation you've already inflicted, and learn to torture us in much better, more beautiful and consenting ways.

How to Dread the Wonderful for Fun and Profit

Most of this book has been about the very important and little-understood *solve* part of the *solve et coagula* formation of magic. I figured I'd leave you with a little *coagula* instruction.

Now, pretty much any instructions on practical magic will encourage you to have "faith" or "trust" in the results of your efforts. But, what if, like me, you *suck* at feeling joyful faith in positive outcomes?

What if your brain is tuned to cynicism and dread? Maybe you've just had a lot of hard-knocks in your life and it's tough to trust that everything will suddenly get all rosy for no reason?

Well, there's a way to leverage that. Faith in an outcome is just a sensation of certainty.

So you can take the very same well-developed brain muscles that you use to get a sensation of certainty about the negative stuff you dread, and turn that around into certainty about positive outcomes.

Here's how: dread the wonderful.

Let's say your magical aim is to have a delightful new romantic partner for the New Year. Now ordinarily most manifestation teachers would tell you to say stuff to yourself like:

"I now affirm that I am receiving my soul's true partner for the highest good of all. I happily look forward to sharing love with this amazing person. I now allow myself to receive new love."

Mmm. Yeah, and has that worked?

I'm gonna go ahead and guess. . . probably not.

You see, as long as we have an inner conflict about/unconscious resistance to such positive affirmation (which you're pretty much guaranteed to have, or else you would have already manifested that precise result) you'll automatically unconsciously negate such happy stuff.

You'll mark it as "nonsense" and not really believe it, even if you're visualizing and affirming it.

Faithful positivity as it's usually taught often has an element of weird denial in it. It isn't as effective as honesty. Honesty is always the best policy, and by Dreading the Wonderful, you bring in the honest, previously-unconscious part of you that despises the happy result you claim to want.

Here's how it works. Try leveraging your dread by saying this to yourself:

> "Oh *no*, if only there was *something I could do* to stop the inevitable arrival of this magnificent new partner in my life. This is so awful. Now I have someone sane and healthy and hot who adores me. It's utterly disgusting. I'm really grieving that my singlehood is coming to this tragic and decisive end. It's just that I'm powerless over this new romance thing; *I just know it's unavoidably going to happen*—ugh. I really wish it was somehow possible for me to escape this relentless, terrifying fate of being completely fulfilled in love."

Ahhhhh, can you feel the honesty there?

Refreshing, isn't it?

Because there *is* some shadowy part of you that's disgusted and miserable at the idea of fresh new love, isn't there?

Otherwise you'd be such a radiant beacon of romance that you'd get swept off the scene in a hot minute.

Well, you can become exactly that radiant beacon of romance by being willing to own and embrace all parts of yourself, including the part that fucking hates the idea of a new gooey *loooooooooooove*.

Of course you can apply the Dreading the Wonderful principle to anything. You can start dreading the inevitable vast improvement of your health, blast-off in creativity, and surge in career and business power.

More Stories of Transformative Experiences

An End to a "Self-Esteem" Problem
—*Elise*

Existential Kink helped me get to the root of what the rest of the world diagnosed as a self-esteem problem. For years, therapists told me that I wasn't assertive enough, that I was too timid, that I didn't express my opinions when I needed to. They never took it further than blaming it on my parents and telling me to start "respecting myself enough to speak up." This advice didn't actually help. It just led me to see myself as weak. (And really, my parents were pretty good, all things considered.)

When I started Existential Kink, I wasn't even thinking about applying it to my "self-esteem problem." I had studied magick for years, but never really managed to integrate it into my life. No matter how many books I read or rituals I performed, life felt mundane, and I couldn't figure out how to change it.

Starting EK, I tried a number of different "strokes" about pretending to be normal, or pretending to live a magick-less life, but none of them really brought the electric thrill that others were describing. After a few weeks of little result, I began to think that this process just wasn't for me.

It took a fight with my partner for me to figure it out. Fortunately, I had been thinking enough about EK (daily) that I had the presence of mind to employ it to any "don't like" moments.

In an argument where I don't even remember the subject (it wasn't remotely important in the end), I again found myself giving in, letting go of my desire, and letting my partner get what they wanted at the expense of my own plans. Instead of feeling disgusted with myself or berating myself for being weak, I relaxed into the feeling and gave myself permission to enjoy it.

And enjoy it I did. The thought "I love being a martyr to other people's decisions" brought an amazing rush of physical pleasure and mental clarity.

On a physical, emotional, and intellectual level, I enjoy being bound by other people's beliefs and desires. It makes me feel self-righteous, and I take a huge amount of pleasure in making them feel guilty over how they've made me a victim. I really, really don't hate to say, "I told you so." Standing up for myself robs me of the opportunity to experience the bliss of martyrdom. (See, therapists? It's not self-esteem.)

Since that realization, I've been much more cognizant of the pattern whenever it arises. That attention has helped me make better choices about when to indulge it (and you really can INDULGE it) and when to set it aside. The more time I spend enjoying it, the less negative impact it has. It's like the emotional center of the pattern has turned from negative to positive, and now I can control it instead of it controlling me.

I can't claim that it's gone completely, but I don't even feel the need to get rid of it anymore. It can fade if it wants. If not, I'll just keep enjoying it when I choose to. Now all that energy that I bound up in fighting myself for "being weak" is free. And I've invested it in a life that is feeling much less mundane than what I had before. I'm far from finished with working on this feeling; I'm sure there's much more I can do. But I use it now as a tool, and it sure is helpful.

Dissolving Old Relationship Patterns
—Megan

I feel so controlled and disregarded and used and abused; so emotionally manipulated, so taken for granted; so disrespected, so ignored, so belittled, so put upon. And it's such a fucking turn-on. I'm not going to pretend any more that I don't enjoy it.

Like so many others, I had this particularly unpleasant relationship gremlin. All my serious relationships had been pretty extreme.

All of them, no matter how different they'd seemed from the outset, always wound up making me feel exactly the same—controlled. Powerless. It actually felt like I didn't have my own life anymore (and 'til I left them, I pretty much didn't).

There would be fights, so many fights, and on a regular basis, as my fury at feeling so oppressed would unleash itself. And things never seemed to change, even when the players did. If anything, with the next player in line, they only got worse.

Most of my partners were creative, free spirits who didn't have jobs. Or didn't have a job at the time I was involved with them. One, I employed myself, but I had to fire him not so long after I hired him and the threats came long and thick. I ran a business with another, for which I put up all the money, and when things went south, I had a pretty tough time trying to cut myself loose. The list went on.

I always figured it had a lot to do with my own poor choices. You know how that story goes, right? I was pretty much sold on it. Of course I'd heard of this 'mirroring' trick that the Universe is known for playing on all her unsuspecting children, something about two people being attracted to each other because there's ultimately some kind of resonance at play, but I'd clearly never quite understood the tenets. My take on it all had been that I simply needed to learn to assert my boundaries better, generally be stronger and wiser about stuff; and (get this!) just make sure I chose differently next time. Ha! ("differently" being a euphemism, the word I meant was "better.")

And I wasn't trying to be ignorant. I genuinely believed it. But here's what I know now: our standards may well need resetting, but so do the stories we tell ourselves. And there simply comes a point where you need to change your record.

When I started doing EK, I was pretty at the point of surrender (why must we get to that point?!). The first time I practiced, it was weird. Imagine my surprise when I lay down on my bed and attempted to really go into these feelings only to realize I was actually getting turned on by it all?! I got carried away. There was more than just a twinge of self-flagellation in all of my scenarios. Let's say I enjoyed it!

As things progressed over the next few weeks, I started to realize that these strange, evocative sensations in my body could actually provide a compelling funnel of focus for me.

This totally fascinated me, not least because I'd barely even noticed these feelings before at all.

I've always been one for over-thinking, so perhaps this was the first time I was truly dropping right down into the body. I'd always found meditation difficult.

But with this newfound focus, and with time, and in this welcome new resulting state of space and clarity that was being birthed via my own, simple enjoyment, I started receiving what I can only describe as insights. I realize now that this is what happens when you just sit with a sensation and allow it to just be. In this state of acceptance and allowance, you generally find that at some point, your curiosity rises, so you begin to look for answers, what happens is. . . you find them! You just have to open up to the possibility first. The possibility that there might be something there that's not just the same old story you've been telling your-self for years.

The first insights I received came to me as memories—memories of all the guys I'd swiftly shut down without even giv-ing them a split second of a chance, let alone a date. Memories of friends wondering why I never went for older guys instead, or ones who were "more successful."

And I remembered other things too: Anyone who was actu-ally available and interested pretty much always got shot down. Anyone with his own money/business in particular, I just wasn't attracted to them. I wished I could be, but I just wasn't. All the men I finally wound up going for were "different" somehow. I'd thought I was a free spirit so that's the kind of guy I thought I should go for. And there was another pattern: one of finding myself in love with men I couldn't quite have.

The curiosity I was invoking through my EK practice was start-ing to make me realize there might well be some cracks in my conscious processing. So, too, were the insights: Having to be all kinds of things to all people makes me feel supremely important, like I am the Queen, and everyone my subjects. My poor wretched people! I never make mistakes, and I've got such a perfect life that I have to help other people and put their needs first, because they aren't as lucky as me.

I feel important and valued and also overcrowded and put upon and smothered, which, I came to realize, turns out not only to be a MASSIVE sexual turn-on, but also a) enables me to avoid putting a lot of time and effort into my creative projects (in case I fail, I am therefore not perfect) and b) enables me to avoid potentially meeting someone who will be right for me (because I never have time, and even when I do, I need to be alone so I can recharge my batteries).

One evening, I cracked wide open. My mind had actually relaxed so much that I simply closed my eyes and fell into a dreamlike state. And there, what I saw was this: an image of a guy who was dressed in something expensive. Let's say a business suit. Then suddenly, and without any warning, his face became clearer. And the image morphed into my father! I instantly recoiled. My eyes flew open.

Because the truth was suddenly icky—too icky to even think about, but now I could see it plainly and clearly, and I couldn't deny it. I had deliberately been choosing and engineering the kind of relationships I'd been involved with because I was scared. Wasn't I? Because, you see, if they didn't need me; let's say, if they were independent and financially successful like my father who left our family had been. . . . No. No. No. Then they might leave me, too.

When you're faced with ugly truths like these, it's fairly hard to forget them. You simply can't keep hiding.

Free spirit? Flighty? Ha! Not really. Terrified of rejection and of being in anything too real, I had painstakingly only sought relationships with those I felt I had power over in some way or other. And so, my dea—who had really been controlling things? Them? Or me?

I pretended I had no control, but really, my situation was precisely managed by me. This way, I don't have to free-flow and actually live life openly and honestly and innocently, and from the heart. This way, I don't have to be vulnerable. Not openly owning this hugely controlling side before has also led to my having projected this quality onto others instead, and I have felt incredibly controlled in past relationships, and in a more extreme way each time.

It's been quite a few months since I did that work. And the million-dollar question: Am I in another relationship yet?

The answer is no—not yet. But I've shifted so much. I feel empowered, excited; amused, grounded, grateful, filled with compassion, and self-compassion. I'd always felt so powerless, and yet the joke was that I'd clearly been wielding the power all along. Because, make no mistake about it, we always have the power, but when it's expressed via our Shadow, unconsciously, it always causes problems. I managed to find the grace to accept my Shadow. And this grace and acceptance, I learned, can be gained from the love we let ourselves feel for the truth that is within our darkest of selves.

After digging so deeply into the patterns I'd spent a lifetime repeating, I think of those past situations almost incredulously now, as though they belong to someone else's life.

In a way, of course, they do.

Airport Magic—*June*

Crowded airports on Friday nights are full of "don't like" situations. My husband and I were traveling to a family wedding—a short trip where we'd attend festivities Saturday and fly home Sunday. But the airline, in its infinite, money-grubbing way, had overbooked our flight. We joined a dozen disgruntled patrons in line to ask for seat assignments. The lady behind the counter shook her head. "You're on the list, but we've got a lot of names in front of you. We might find one or both of you a seat, but certainly not two together." We sat in the terminal, watching the information screens as the list of standby names lengthened with each passing minute.

For at least the third time in a year, my husband swore we'd never fly on this airline again. I didn't have the heart to respond. This was a proper mess. This was the last evening flight, and anything tomorrow morning would get us there too late. How had we gotten into such an annoying situation? We should have sprung for economy-plus seats. We should have checked in online. We should have prayed to Mercury for a smooth journey. We should have . . .

"Having is evidence of wanting," chanted a little voice in the back of my head.

I'd been working with Existential Kink for over a month. It had helped me recognize how much I adored playing martyr to the demands of others. I spent huge amounts of energy working myself into situations where I could say things like, "I want to go meditate right now, but my husband wants to watch a movie together, and I'm so nice and thoughtful and saintly, that I'll give up what I want to make him happy, then . . ." and here my mental monologue usually took on the voice of Scar from the Lion King, ". . . I'll secretly stew in resentment and plan my passive-aggressive revenge in dark, solitary silence. MUAHAHA!"

I'd been lovingly indulging that pattern for weeks now. It had grown into an old, shabby horse-hair coat, or a ridiculous but adorable accessory I could snuggle up in or lay aside depending on the situation. Could this bungled weekend really be the result of my now-beloved personality quirk?

Perhaps not. Perhaps this was something a little different. I took a deep breath and thought very deliberately, how I completely love and accept that I hate flying, and don't want to get onto this plane.

I waited for any sort of internal sensation, but my body felt the same blend of tension and worry as before. Or perhaps there was something in the pit of my stomach . . .? No, I was just hungry.

A different stroke, then. I completely love and accept that I don't want to go to this wedding.

A warm, red flame sprang up inside my chest—a flare of satisfaction and relief. I was so shocked that I spoke aloud.

"Oh!"

"What?" asked my husband.

It was so obvious. We're always doing magic. This powerful rush of pleasure made it clear: I'd manifested this lack of seating. "I did this." I rubbed at my cheeks to cover my flush. It wouldn't do to look excited in front of the TSA.

My husband shook his head. "It's not your fault, honey, it's the stupid airline. Their idea of customer service is so warped . . ." I ignored him. (I'd been getting better at that since recognizing my martyr complex.) I focused on the warm flame inside me, glowing somewhere just beneath my heart.

I treasure my weekends. I love my lazy mornings reading in bed and my long afternoons communing with my tarot cards. I love forgetting about my day job, and having enough time to do what I want, when I want. I love waking up in the middle of the night to drink mugwort tea and savoring the trippy dreams that follow. Since I wasn't going to be traveling, I could do all of that. My lips actually curled into a smile. I turned away so my husband wouldn't see it.

Time to stoke the flame. I was going to make this the best weekend ever. As I reviewed the possibilities, the tingling warmth diffused through my chest and down my legs and arms. Why had I even agreed to go to the wedding in the first place? I was going to make this my time, filled with indulgence and pleasure and lovely solitary pursuits. Maybe I'd throw in a movie to watch with my husband, so I could savor feeling generous and deliciously put-upon. I wouldn't have to see all the boring relatives, or coerce my husband into dancing with me or . . .

. . . Or see my mother. I wouldn't be seeing my mom.

One little ice-cube dropped into the warm sea. A sputter in the flame. I obviously didn't want to go to the wedding. But I had been looking forward to seeing my mom. She'd been through a tough time lately, with the death of a friend and a family member's sickness. My absence would just add to her upset.

I sighed and turned back to my husband. "What are we doing next weekend?" He frowned. "Megan's housewarming party."

"I don't want to go. I'd like to have a free weekend after this."

"That's fair," he shrugged. "I can show up for the both of us."

I nodded and glanced at the information screens. Over forty people on the standby list. Would I really be able to turn this around so late in the game? No harm in trying.

I turned my attention inward. I can have everything I want next weekend. *Desire evolves through fulfillment*, and I'll fulfill that in full. This weekend, I'm going to go see mom. I pictured my mother in my mind. I imagined how she would smile when she saw me, and how it would feel when she hugged me hello.

The warmth faded, but so did the little ice cube in its center. In their place, I felt a soft comfort, like my threadbare childhood blanket. It wasn't as sexy or indulgent as playing hooky, but it was still good. Knowing I wouldn't miss my chance at solitary revels, I could honestly want this with all my heart.

So now I know what I want, I thought. Time to ask for it.

As I focused on my goal—the goal I really, really wanted—something shifted inside me. I felt buoyant, almost mischievous. I was totally going to witch this. We were going to land two seats on a crowded plane, and it would be awesome.

The woman at the desk called my name ten minutes later. "A couple just phoned and said they weren't going to make the flight. You and your husband can have these." She handed me two boarding passes for a pair of seats in an exit row. For the first time in our conversations, she smiled. "It's like it was meant to be."

"I guess so. Thank you."

So it was a weekend of carrot juice, mimosas, middling poetry, and good mother/daughter time. Plus, I got to feel indulgently put-upon as I sat through the boring wedding ceremony, a blissful martyr to family obligations.

As creepy uncle Aleister Crowley said, "Magick is the science and art of causing change to occur in conformity with will." When I needed to figure out where my will was pointing, my deep dark desires were there to lead the way.

Part Three

Questions & Answers

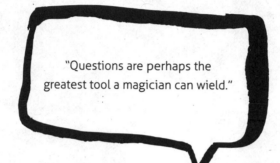

"Questions are perhaps the
greatest tool a magician can wield."

—EK

I n what follows, I answer some common questions that arise for people who are new to the practice of Existential Kink.

. . .

Q. If I enjoy a sucky situation in my life to the point of "getting off on it," why wouldn't I just keep the sucky situation going since I like it so much?

A. Well, you certainly could if you decided to. Or you could decide to take all the energy you had previously been putting into hating and resenting the situation and put it towards creating a fresh adventure for yourself.

The value of wildly, wickedly, shamelessly enjoying "don't like" situations in our lives through the practice of Existential Kink is that we recover our sense of agency and volition. Rather than feeling hopelessly stuck with conditions we detest, we begin to be aware that the conditions are a kinky game we've (unknowingly) created.

As we bring conscious awareness and massive joyful embrace (rather than blaming or shaming ourselves) to that previously unconscious process of creation, we stop identifying with the sucky conditions; we stop feeling like *they define us*.

And this is crucial, because what humans defend more fiercely than anything else is their sense of identity.

A practice of Existential Kink meditation helps to get under those tight defenses and switch things around for the better.

You see, when we suffer from our problems, what we're usually suffering from, much more so than from the direct pain of the problem itself, is the story in our heads that "I'm so awful, I've failed so much, I deserve this, that's why I'm not earning more/happy in love/content in my body/thriving in my creativity."

As you do Existential Kink, you might start to notice that that story of "deserving" yucky stuff is just plain untrue. Nothing in your life is there because you *deserve* it; it's there because you (at some level) *enjoy* it. The universe isn't a balance sheet of worthiness; it's a work of art. Manifestation happens aesthetically, not morally.

When you let yourself feel some vigorous, funny, freaky joy over your problems, the sensations of pain may still be present, but you're now no longer suffering from the sense of "deserving" it or being trapped by it, because it's clear that you just sneakily generated the scene as a form of dark entertainment, and you are actually free to let yourself be fully, consciously satisfied by your artful tragedy. . . and then move on to turning your life into a sweet comedy.

Think for a minute how dark entertainments tend to be the ones that people get most excited about. Two of the most popular TV series in the world at the time of me writing this book, for example, are *Game of Thrones* and *The Walking Dead*. Both shows feature big piles of violence, grief, pain, and horror. There are also heroines and heroes striving epically against all odds to survive and help others to survive as well. These shows are terrifying and people *love* them.

So if we humans love dark pain and horror as entertainment *soooo* much, don't you think it's just a little bit possible that we might unconsciously create painful and horrible situations in our own lives—not because we "deserve them" or because we're "losers" and "failures," but just because we have an attraction to the nail-biting intensity of it?

If there was a TV show about healthy people who were totally happy, thriving in all of their work and relationships, with no problems or challenges, absolutely no one would watch it. Even in wholesome comedies there are obstacles and dilemmas that create tension and hilarity.

· · ·

Q. My favorite Law of Attraction teacher says that if I focus on painful things in my life, then I'll make them bigger, but if I focus on the positive things that I want, then I'll attract those positive things. How will doing Existential Kink not just make the painful situations in my life bigger?

A. Existential Kink practice is totally compatible with Law of Attraction teachings; actually, I consider it at heart to be "the next level" of those kinds of teachings.

Because here's the thing: as far as I can discern, the Law of Attraction crowd is completely right about the whole "we are vibrational beings who draw to us circumstances that match our emotional energy" thing.

If you're a habitually miserable, self-pitying person, odds are *very, very* high that you will find yourself with more and more things to be miserable and self-pitying about; and if you're a grateful, enthusiastic person, the odds are also quite high that you'll find yourself with more and more things to be grateful and enthusiastic about.

So I'm in complete agreement with that bit; I have definitely found it true in my own experience and observation. The thing is, I also found that many of the practices popularly taught by Law of Attraction teachers to "raise your vibration" are much too short-lived in their emotional and psychological impact to be actually useful for helping me make long-term shifts.

As in: Some years back, I was a miserable, self-pitying person and no amount of positive visualization or affirmation was doing jack-shit to change that for more than a week or two at a time. So I was continuing to draw to myself more and more things to be self-pitying and miserable about.

Also, the common Law of Attraction advice to just ignore the stuff that bothers you ("Only focus on what you like!") always seemed a bit impossible for me; plus it felt like really strange denial. Like, I'm supposed to affirm that I'm rich while my bank account has minus fifty dollars in it? Will my landlord accept my assurance that the cash to pay the rent is in "vibrational escrow"? Do the utility companies give a fuck that I'm great at visualizing myself receiving fat checks? No, of course not, and this piece of the Law of Attraction practice always struck me as dishonest and dissatisfying.

Existential Kink has a way of deeply shifting your emotional vibration, *permanently*, in a manner that uses profound self-honesty instead of weirdo denial.

If you were meditating on the "don't like" situations in your life only to focus on how really, truly awful and impossible they are and how much you personally suck for having them in your life, then yes, that would indeed be "dwelling on the negative," wallowing in it, even, expanding those feelings of misery and self-pity and that would be *no bueno*.

But if you're bringing a "don't like" situation to mind in order to practice giving yourself deep permission to feel hot, nasty, electric joy about it, well then, that's quite a bit different, isn't it? Because in this later scenario, you aren't wallowing in negativity; you're *wallowing in hot electric bliss*.

And "bliss" is a pretty damn high-vibe emotion, wouldn't you say?

So, speaking in Law of Attraction terms, Existential Kink is actually an immensely useful tool for getting into emotional states that are very conducive to positive manifestation.

Furthermore, when you first get into hot electric kinky bliss about some romantic rejection or career humiliation (or whatever) that your unconscious shadow generated, you are getting into amazingly *honest* bliss, because you're being genuinely truthful with yourself.

Hell yeah, I generated this! Hell yeah, a part of me fucking loves it and that part of me deserves to enjoy itself too, because every part of me is worthy and awesome, including the perverse shadowy parts!

This kind of amazingly honest bliss is a lot more permanent and fully transformative. Why?

Because once you let yourself see the truth of it, you can't ever *unsee* it, your perspective has been forever changed, you can never go back to feeling sorry for yourself because you've *seen through your own game*. So then the next time you find yourself feeling a bit humiliated or rejected, you'll probably also find yourself feeling grateful and turned on, because you know your shadow *loves this shit*, and your shadow is getting beautifully fulfilled.

The honest, permanently transformative bliss we're talking about here is also a lot more vibrationally potent than some kind of brief high created by only looking on the bright side of your life. That kind of Pollyanna high can be immediately dashed to pieces the moment you forget to keep up your avoidance of stark realities (the landlord knocks on the door; you notice the object of your unrequited affection out on a date with someone else, etc. etc.).

So Existential Kink is different from the conventional Law of Attraction approach in that it says: *don't* ignore or deny those stark realities, go right into 'em with tons of shameless sadomasochistic glee, enjoy the fuck out of 'em, and be honestly happy instead of weird-denial-fake-happy.

Then, as you enjoy your honest happiness, you'll notice that brilliant solutions and avenues of opportunity tend to open up in ways they never have before. While you're luxuriating in this happiness, I suggest trying some creative visualizations for new things you'd like to create in your life. Visualization works a lot better after you've been kinkily real with yourself.

. . .

Q. I don't feel anything at all when I try to do Existential Kink. What's going on?

A. You might need to relax more before attempting the Existential Kink practice. Try taking a hot bath and taking some deep belly breaths to help you become more present in your body; then try the Existential Kink meditation again.

If relaxation doesn't help, this is usually either an issue of depression (in which case, see the next question and answer below) or of some kind of intense sexual repression issue. If you can't allow yourself to feel pleasurable sexual sensations, this is a matter beyond what a book can help you with.

I highly encourage you to seek out well-regarded therapists and bodyworkers who are experienced with addressing sexual trauma and helping patients allow themselves to experience sensation.

. . .

Q. I'm depressed, it's hard for me to feel anything when I try to do Existential Kink, and sometimes I think my attempts may make me kinda feel worse. What do I do?

A. My great sympathies to you. I've struggled with depression many times in my life, and I know it's brutal.

As I mentioned in the introduction to the Basic Existential Kink practice, I *do not* recommend attempting to do Existential Kink practice while depressed because in my experience and observation, it can result in rumination and self-flagellation (not the fun kind).

You see, in order for "get off" to happen in EK, in order for the intense sensations of a "don't like" situation to get alchemized into hot electric joy, there needs to be *some* amount of free-floating good energy and good humor already present in your system. It's kind of like how you need oxygen to be present in order to spark a fire. Good humor, good energy, is like oxygen to the spark of EK practice.

Depression tends to be a condition of not being able to take pleasure in *anything*, let alone your freaky perverse unconscious desires and manifestations. However, just because you're depressed and EK may not be the best tool for you at this time, this does *not* mean that you can't do the *solve* process of making the unconscious, conscious and thereby uniting your will. Deepest Fear Inventory and Inquiry are very excellent *solve* practices that can help you remove layers of bullshit and raise your spirits, and they work great while depressed.

When I've been depressed, The Work of Byron Katie inquiry practice has helped me immensely. We humans tend to make ourselves depressed by believing bleak narratives about ourselves and other people. When you question these, often the heavy feelings tend to lift. So, definitely do that. See the Appendix for more information on The Work.

I also (speaking as a human being and not as any kind of psychologist or medical professional, since I'm not those) recommend practicing Brahmavihara meditation as an antidote to depression.

The book *Love 2.0: Finding Happiness and Health in Moments of Connection* does an excellent job of explaining how to do the

Metta sort of Brahmavihara meditation, which involves sending powerful well-wishes to others.

I know sending well-wishes may not sound like that dramatically transformative of a meditation (and it doesn't have the sexy swagger of EK, alas), but in my experience and the experience of thousands of my course participants, it is indeed a rapid way of shifting one's emotional energy, clearing out resentment and cynicism, and getting in touch with the giant power of your heart.

Also, if you're depressed I suggest that you check out EFT (Emotional Freedom Technique), which involves tapping on acupressure points while saying helpful statements. You can also easily find demonstrations of this process on YouTube.

Finally, I suggest that you read *The Mood Cure* by Julia Ross and follow the protocol she recommends for your particular condition, as depression issues are often hormonal and Ross has well-researched supplement suggestions for most forms of mood problems. I've greatly benefitted from following her protocols myself.

I wish you the very best good fortune in lifting yourself out of depression. I know it can be a harrowing journey; know that Existential Kink will still be here for you once you've got some of that aforementioned free-floating good and humorous energy swirling around in your body.

· · ·

Q. I can definitely feel some strong electric sensations when I do EK, but so far nothing close to climaxing. Am I doing this right?

A. Yes, you are totally doing it right. When I talk about "getting off" in EK, I mean experiencing pretty much any kind of pleasure surrounding a topic that previously only brought frustration.

This could be a sexual climax experienced genitally; or it could be sensations of electricity moving in the body; or it could be an emotion of simple relief or of joy and laughter.

Often "getting off" in EK does include some kind of peak that resembles a climax of sort, but other times the sensation of lift, pleasure, and lightness is more diffuse and subtle.

Also, keep in mind: depending on the issue, it may take you a few hours, days, weeks, or even months of practice before you're able to relax fully enough to give yourself permission to "get off." Even if it takes you months, remember, that's still a relatively *very brief* span of time and effort to permanently change a life-long negative pattern. Consider that most human beings only shift their negative patterns after years of therapy or, you know, *never*. So even if it seems to you that your EK process is going slow, know that you're still in the fast lane.

Also, some "don't like" situations you will find are much easier to get off on than others. Which kind of "don't like" situation is easiest to get off on varies widely from person-to-person. For example, for me it only took a couple of weeks to get off on my financial scarcity issues, but it took about six months to get off on my romance stuff, because I had more shame around it and it took more persistence to gently set that aside.

Others might find that the reverse is true for them. You'll know that you've successfully "gotten off" on a situation with EK when thinking about or encountering the situation feels genuinely (not sardonically or ironically) fun, intriguing, and pleasurable to you.

. . .

Q. The "don't like" situation I have in my life right now is utterly terrible and soul-crushing. I don't see how I could ever derive pleasure, let alone sexual pleasure, from it. It's too awful. What do I do?

A. I hear you.

It may be that the most pressing "don't like" situation in your life is a too-daunting place to begin. This is often the case when there's still grief to move through.

As my friends Leslie Rogers and Tanni Thole teach in their wonderful Light/Dark Institute workshops, humans tend to experience the sensations of life through an emotional spectrum that ranges from hedonistic pleasure to profound grief. Plenty of us have a hard time going fully into grief, but it's very important to do because if you don't fully feel your grief, you can never fully feel your pleasure.

If the "don't like" situation you're facing now in your life isn't simply frustrating or embarrassing but rather cuts to the quick of your soul with immense sorrow, then fully grieving the situation should be your first priority.

For example, let's say your biggest "don't like" situation is that you recently found out your husband cheated on you with your best friend. Now I'm a sadistic freak, but I would never suggest that anyone go straight to practicing EK on something like that. And this goes for all varieties of life experience that involve tremendous feelings of loss.

In these kinds of situations, I would suggest that you devote tons of time to classic grieving. Really feel those feelings; find a great therapist and tell her all about it; reach out to family and other friends for support; drink a lot of chamomile tea; take hot baths; make appointments with yourself to listen to music and cry, cry, cry.

The Existential Kink approach to life is absolutely not about denial; it's about fully feeling what's honestly there.

So if immense grief and feelings of betrayal are what's there, then go all the way into it, mourn in the most profound ways you can. Wear all black. Make performance art about it. Burn effigies of your betrayers. Whatever you gotta do.

While going through this process, if you really want, you can certainly practice EK on much more mild "don't like" scenarios in your life (such as annoying co-workers; your car needing to go to the shop; finding your favorite sweater has been eaten by moths during the winter). This can help give you fluency with the EK process so that you gradually trust it to help you with deeper matters.

With time, as the intensity of your immediate grief fades, I would suggest doing The Work of Byron Katie inquiry process on your judgments about the situation, yourself, your husband, your best friend.

I would then suggest writing a Deepest Fear Inventory on topics like "Dear Universe, I hate and resent having totally trustworthy and transparent people in my life . . . because I have deep fear that I . . ."

After you feel you've gained plenty of peace and perspective from classic grieving, inquiry, and DFI, and have good feelings and good humor again circulating in your body, then, and *only then*, would I suggest gently exploring EK on the matter.

· · ·

Q. My life right now is okay but I know it would be better if I wasn't burdened by all the childhood trauma issues that I have. Should I do EK on my childhood trauma stuff?

A. Short answer: no.

I understand that once you learn about how the unconscious creates painful life situations it can be very tempting to go right to the most hurtful wounds you ever experienced and try to get off on them. I do not recommend this at all.

First, doing EK practice on milder "don't like" situations in your present life will itself go an amazingly long way towards resolving your frustrations and opening up much more happiness, beauty, and bounty in your world.

Second of all, trying to do EK on intense traumas in your past is like trying to do EK while depressed: it tends to just lead to rumination, and that is not helpful.

Third of all, things get quite strange when one starts to discuss how a child's unconscious might draw them into specific painful situations.

For myself, after long years of pondering it, visions in meditation, and decades of skepticism, I've come to feel that my own soul was indeed curious about and drawn to specific very painful childhood experiences, and thus my soul chose to incarnate with my parents in order to undergo those experiences, but I'm not interested in asking readers of this book to accept such far-out metaphysical beliefs about themselves.

The simple observable fact is: as children we are quite powerless in our choice of surroundings and companions; as adults we have immense power in our choice of surroundings.

So I think it's far preferable to do EK on what you have created for yourself as an adult who is free to navigate in the world, rather than doing EK on what you experienced as a dependent and powerless child.

And even this has caveats: first of all, many adult experiences just need plenty of grieving to be fully felt and handled, and second, as we discussed in Lesson 2 (The Seven Axioms of Existential Kink), many painful situations, like those involving racism and sexism and child abuse, entail elements that emerge primarily from the *collective unconscious*, rather than from just your own *personal unconscious*.

What I like about doing EK on frustrating situations in your *present* life is that to get great freedom from your old negative patterns you don't need to figure out fuzzy spiritual matters like karma and reincarnation; you can just work with well-established psychological truths—specifically, the psychological truth that we all have repressed sadomasochistic shadow desires for things that our conscious mind and ego heavily disapprove of, including jolly classics like patterns of financial scarcity, romantic rejection, and creative blocks.

Third, traumas require immense grieving. See the Q&A above about EK and grief.

Reminder: I am not a psychologist or a medical professional. That said, as another human being who has suffered trauma, I suggest plenty of regular ole' therapy, exploring bodywork and acupuncture, gathering tons of support from friends, and moving heaven and earth to get thyself to many ayahuasca ceremonies and to legal MDMA therapy sessions if you can find them.

Ayahuasca is the most useful, beautiful, and rapid means I know of for addressing deep trauma (it has helped me immensely), and studies have shown that MDMA in a therapeutic context is also quite powerful for resolving trauma. I am proposing that you con-sider using these kinds of intense entheogenic substances only in well-held spaces with experienced healers, not just because I'm a giant hippie, but because they work.

Trauma is very difficult to resolve, and while regular therapy is quite important for helping you to handle the day-to-day chal-lenge of living life with such a wound, it remains the case that talk therapy is limited in its ability to get to the core of a trauma and heal it.

This is why entheogens, used properly and wisely, are wonderful.

Ayahuasca is not currently legal in the United States, so this means if you want to pursue it, you need to get yourself to South America.

My friends Pam and Brown at the Avatar Centre in Peru are quite experienced and excellent ceremony leaders, and I very strongly recommend (speaking as a human, not a psychologist or medical professional) seeking their help. Obviously international travel takes money, time, and planning but I do believe it is absolutely worth it if you strongly desire to resolve your trauma.

Appendix

My favorite warm-up for Existential Kink and the practice I turn to when I'm not in a good mood and so not really ready to do Existential Kink is Inquiry. Inquiry is a contemplative process of asking oneself probing questions about one's own perception and listening inwardly for answers. It's a very good habit to cultivate, because as we've seen, our perceptions are highly suspect and conditioned by our unconscious and by our cultural surroundings.

My favorite processes of Inquiry include:

1) The Work of Byron Katie
You can find free information on how to do The Work at *thework .com.* You can also find tons of videos on YouTube of Byron Katie leading people through the process.

   If The Work interests you, I suggest that you invest in Byron Katie's books, *Loving What Is* and *A Thousand Names for Joy.*

2) The Option Method
Similar to the Work but less well-known, the Option Method also involves investigating one's habitual perceptions. You can find instructions on the Option Method at *www.optionmethodnetwork .com.*

3) The Sedona Method
This form of Inquiry is perhaps the most direct of the bunch, focused on "letting go" of difficult emotions. You can find the basic instructions for the Sedona Method at *www.sedona.com.*

If the Sedona Method interests you, I also recommend buying and reading *The Sedona Method* book because it contains more detailed context and perspective that makes the practice more helpful.

David Hawkins' book *Letting Go: The Pathway of Surrender* also focuses on principles related to the Sedona Method.

Advice for Inquiry

My general advice for practicing any form of Inquiry is to approach the practice with a willingness to set aside everything you think you know to be true and to simply investigate with a radically open mind.

Gradually, with Inquiry, you might discover that when a statement or proposition is true for you it feels different in your body than a fictional statement. True statements (or your being giving an affirmative answer to a question) tends to feel warm, soft, expansive, resonant, and open in the heart. Untrue statements (or your being giving a negative answer to a question) tend to feel tight, heavy, weakening, and constricting.

For example, in doing the Work, if I write down a judgment and ask myself "Is it true?" (the first question of the Work) and find only a tight, heavy, weak, and constricted feeling in my body, that's a clue to me that the judgment is not true, that it's an unhappy fiction.

Truth often has a beautiful throb of resonance to it that untruth lacks.

If later in the process I ask myself "Who would I be without that thought?" (the fourth question of the Work) and find a warm, soft, expansive, and open feeling in my body, then that's a clue to me that there's more truth to letting go of the thought than there is to holding onto it.

Often the mind will go blank when you ask yourself a question in Inquiry. And that's okay. For example, sometimes while doing the Option Method I ask myself "What would it mean about me if I wasn't unhappy about that?"and my mind just draws a blank. I don't know what it would mean. But just the action of asking the question draws my attention to the fact that being unhappy about something *is a subtle unconscious choice that I habitually make* and it's a subtle choice that I can make conscious and change, thus changing my fate.

So just the action of asking the question, of doing the Inquiry, is always valuable, even if I can't immediately find an answer. Questions about the nature of our perceptions and reactions are perhaps the greatest tool a magician can wield, because they shine the light of attention, bringing consciousness to what was previously unconscious.

PHOTO BY BELLATRIX PHOTOGRAPHY | CAMILA MENDES

About the Author

Carolyn Elliott, PhD, is an author and teacher who specializes in helping people achieve dramatic positive change in their lives through shadow integration practices and applied occult philosophy. She founded the online Witch magazine (*www. badwitch.es*) to give voice to the subtle "witching" in the world that's not confined to tradition and convention, and she is cohost of the Grit & Grace podcast with her partner Taia Kepher. Carolyn is the creator of several popular online courses including INFLUENCE, FORCE OF NATURE, MONEY, LOVE, and THRILL. She earned her PhD in Critical and Cultural Studies from the University of Pittsburgh, and also writes poetry, plays, and fiction. She resides in her hometown of Pittsburgh, Pennsylvania, with her family.

For more information on workshops and coaching, please contact Carolyn at *www.carolyngraceelliott.com.*

Existential Kink Resources

People learn the most about Existential Kink in conversation with others doing the practice.

To connect with folks around the world changing their lives with Existential Kink, please join the Existential Kink Facebook Group where you can share about your experiences and learn from others.

To join us, visit *www.facebook.com/groups/existentialkink*, click "request to join," and you'll be added to the group within a week.

To receive a download of a free guided Existential Kink meditation recorded by the author, please visit *www.existentialkink.com* and enter your email address.

To Our Readers

Weiser Books, an imprint of Red Wheel/Weiser, publishes books across the entire spectrum of occult, esoteric, speculative, and New Age subjects. Our mission is to publish quality books that will make a difference in people's lives without advocating any one particular path or field of study. We value the integrity, originality, and depth of knowledge of our authors.

Our readers are our most important resource, and we appreciate your input, suggestions, and ideas about what you would like to see published.

Visit our website at *www.redwheelweiser.com* to learn about our upcoming books and free downloads, and be sure to go to *www.redwheelweiser.com/newsletter* to sign up for newsletters and exclusive offers.

You can also contact us at *info@rwwbooks.com* or at

Red Wheel/Weiser, LLC
65 Parker Street, Suite 7
Newburyport, MA 01950